I found the book useful as a sort of 'a la carte' menu where I could piece together a complete marketing plan for my next big project. Thanks Marisa for finally putting such a great breadth of material neatly together in one place.

—Diane K. Danielson, Executive Director of Downtown Women's Clubs and Coauthor of *Table Talk: The Savvy Girl's Alternative to Networking*

This is more than a book—it's a course, a workbook, a graduate-level education from a savvy publicist willing to share her secrets. Marisa D'Vari shows you how to approach and enchant the media, become the go-to expert in your field, and enhance your business with public speaking and writing. D'Vari is clever, resourceful, and up to date. She'll teach you how to break in with a bang.

—Joan Price, Author of *The Anytime, Anywhere Exercise Book: 300+ Quick and Easy Exercises You Can Do Whenever You Want!*

The Holy Grail of marketing and PR is the creation of buzz. Read this book! Do as Marisa advises! She has the inside track on the elusive-but-powerful concept of buzz.

—Gregory J.P. Godek, Author of *1001 Ways To Be Romantic*

If the reader follows the Building Buzz path, success will be there at the end.

—Nance Mitchell, Founder of Nance Mitchell Company

Marisa has included everything you'd ever need to know to create buzz for your project. Having appeared on Oprah, 60 Minutes, NPR, and been Microsoft's spokesperson, I know that what she outlines works! She gives you a soup-to-nuts recipe for success!

—Rebecca Morgan, CSP, CMC,
Best-Selling Author,
Speaker, and Management
Consultant

Filled with colorful anecdotes and clever assignments to drive the message home, D'Vari provides an easy-to-read tool that will help anyone attract the media's attention quickly and easily.

—Dan Janal, Founder of PR LEADS Expert
Resource Network

Building Buzz is chock-full of ideas to help you leverage your expertise in the marketplace. It works as a quick-study guide for those just starting out, and a valuable refresher course for those already successful (or on their way to success!) in their chosen field.

—Mary Lou Andre, Author of *Ready to Wear:
An Expert's Guide to Choosing and
Using Your Wardrobe*

This book is packed with 'eureka!' moments. You'll dramatically cut your learning curve and instantly start building buzz by reading just one book. Leave it to Marisa to deliver an illuminating work that's so complete it feels like cheating!

—Connie Dieken, President of
Communicate Like a Pro

Most women I work with simply don't know how to promote their careers—how to 'brag on themselves.' This little book will help them get out the good word about their wonderful accomplishments. Marisa's plan makes it easy—and comfortable—for us to really impress our special audiences!

—Jane Breschard Wilson, Founder of
Boston Women Communicators

Marisa D'Vari is the Baroness of Buzz. Here, in one compact volume, are all the media tricks it has taken the rest of us a lifetime to learn. Smart, savvy and well organized, this book will tell you in a few hours the information you'd pay a fortune to get from a PR expert.

—Tina B. Tessina, Ph.D., Speaker,
Psychotherapist, and Author of
It Ends With You

Concise, clear, comprehensive, and current—Building Buzz is crammed with exactly the kind of advice I've been giving my marketing clients for the past 30 years. Particularly strong on media coaching and on building your personal spiral of expertise—areas that are rarely covered properly in most marketing books.

—Shel Horowitz, Author of
*Grassroots Marketing:
Getting Noticed in a Noisy World* and Owner of
FrugalMarketing.com

A crash course in self-promotion that really works.

—Paula Munier, Author of *On Being Blonde*
and Director of Product Development
for Adams Media

Marisa D'Vari's Building Buzz *is excellent. It defines a step-by-step path to create your platform, validate it to those who care (or should), and let them help you succeed. My focus is on empire-building through niche publishing and marketing. Zero in on Marisa's message. Doing what she says makes niching all that more productive and profitable.*

—Gordon Burgett, Author of 1,700 articles
and 27 books, including
Publishing to Niche Markets and *Empire-Building
for Writers and Speakers*

Anyone with a product, service, book, or business will benefit from reading this incredible book. Packed with advice, tips, tricks, and secrets to success, Building Buzz *is a gold mine of information. Grab a highlighter, take copious notes, and let media expert Marisa D'Vari show you how to take any business from ordinary to extraordinary.*

—Penny C. Sansevieri, Founder of
Marketing Experts, Inc.

Building Buzz *needs to be at the fingertips of every success-seeking entrepreneur and professional. It's loaded with practical, doable strategies to grow your business. Actual samples of proven e-mails—and the 'why' behind them—make this an indispensable resource. Marisa D'Vari is a savvy media magician.*

—Marilyn Ross, Consultant, Speaker, and Author
of *Jump Start Your Book Sales* and *Shameless
Marketing for Brazen Hussies*

Building Buzz *is a must-read manual for anyone who wants to create value and capture the light of fame. Brimming with success stories and easy bite-size steps, D'Vari generously shares her trade secrets and coaches you on how to achieve them. It is an indispensable resource that you will want to read and reread as you climb the ladder of success.*

—Bonnie Carson DiMatteo, President of
Atlantic Consulting

As a successful self-published author, I thought I knew a thing or two about building buzz. Then I read this amazing, information-rich, cover-all-the-bases, spell-it-all-out resource. The first 10 pages has more good stuff than most entire books.

—Peter Bowerman,
Author of *The Well-Fed Writer*

Building Buzz *is required reading for any professional who wants more visibility and credibility within the marketplace. I wish I had this book when I started consulting 20 years ago. It would have saved me a lot of time and money. I'm glad I have this book now. Marisa offers nuggets of wisdom for everyone—no matter what your experience level!*

—Cindy Ventrice,
Author of *Make Their Day!:
Employee Recognition That Works*

Marisa D'Vari knows all the secrets of how to promote yourself on radio, TV, and in print. She really knows her stuff.

—William A. Gordon, Author, Publisher, and Editor of "Gordon's Radio List"

Bull's-eye! Once again Marisa's media expertise takes you by the hand to get the press shouting all about you and your story. Building Buzz can have the media talking about the most important person in your business—you.

—John Fuhrman, Author and Speaker

Marisa D'Vari's Building Buzz is a wonderful potpourri of publicity tips—everything from crafting a killer speech to promoting via an e-zine, from pitching editors to publishing books. If you're trying to impress your target audience, this is an invaluable resource.

—Fern Reiss, CEO of Expertizing.com/ PublishingGame.com

Marisa D'Vari has done it again! The winning combination—her crisp writing style and insight into a complex culture that she truly understands—is responsible for creating a book that is packed with helpful information, tested tools that work, and powerful strategies any savvy professional would want to use. Read this book!

—Mr. Lloyd Sheldon Johnson, Black Star Enterprises

If you want to take your business to another level without spending a lot of money you don't have, I have three suggestions…Read this book! Read this book! Read this book! Marisa provides a comprehensive template in encouraging, easy-to-understand language that is guaranteed to change how you do business. Until now, my business has been all word of mouth. As I read the book, I began implementing some of her suggestions and within days I'm experiencing results! This is a must-read for any small business owner who wants to establish themselves as the go-to resource in their field!

—Geri Amori, Ph.D., Founder of
Communicating HealthCare

I love this! Anyone wanting to know how to get their name and face in the news and to win new clients by getting famous NEEDS this gem right now. Brilliant!

—Dr. Joe Vitale, Author of *The Attractor Factor*

Tells you everything you need to know about building buzz, but didn't know who to ask.

—Robin Quinn, Award-Winning Author and
Former Associate Producer of NBC News

Marisa has done it again! Building Buzz is packed with information on how to be a media darling. Make no mistake, if you take the time to implement Marisa's words of wisdom, you will impress the market of your dreams.

—MyLinda Butterworth, Conference Coordinator,
Florida Publishers Association

Building Buzz

How to Reach and Impress Your Target Audience

By

Marisa D'Vari

Foreword
by
Susan RoAne
Author of *How to Work a Room*

CAREER
PRESS
Franklin Lakes, NJ

BUILDING BUZZ
EDITED BY GINA M. CHESELKA
TYPESET BY EILEEN DOW MUNSON
Cover design by Cheryl Cohan Finbow
Printed in the U.S.A. by Book-mart Press

To order this title, please call toll-free 1-800-CAREER-1 (NJ and Canada: 201-848-0310) to order using VISA or MasterCard, or for further information on books from Career Press.

The Career Press, Inc., 3 Tice Road, PO Box 687,
Franklin Lakes, NJ 07417
www.careerpress.com

Library of Congress Cataloging-in-Publication Data
D'Vari, Marisa.
  Building buzz : how to reach and impress your target audience / by Marisa D'Vari ; foreword by Susan Roane.
    p. cm.
  Includes index.
  ISBN 1-56414-779-7 (pbk.)
  1. Advertising media planning. 2. Advertising. 3. Publicity. 4. Public relations. I. Title.

HF5826.5.D86 2004
659.1'11--dc21

2004056561

For Ron D'Vari:

far too gorgeous, lively, and fun for a man possessing such dazzling brilliance.

And, *of course*, to the Mi and Apricat!

Acknowledgments

A special thanks to:

Colleen Mohyde, thanks for being such a great agent. Much appreciation to Michael Pye, Kirsten Beucler, Gina Cheselka, Stacey Farkas, Linda Rienecker, Eileen Munson, and the entire Career Press team.

Several individuals were generous enough to give extensive interviews that helped make this book a success. Thank you to everyone who contributed to this book, especially Debbie Allen, Mary Lou Andre, Judith Appelbaum, John Boe, Nicholas Boothman, Peter Bowerman, Gordon Burgett, Jack Canfield, Ken Winston Caine, William Corcoron, Diane Danielson, Diane Darling, Paulette Ensign, Carl Friesen, John Fuhrman, Janet Lang, Debbi Karpowicz-Kickham, Mark Victor Hanson, Lenny Laskowski, Margery Mayer, Nancy Michaels, Rebecca Morgan, Paula Munier, Jan Nathan, Thomas Plante, Ph.D, Dan Poynter, Fern Reiss, Marilyn and Tom Ross, Penny Sansevieri, Mr. Lloyd-Sheldon Johnson, Jen Singer, Cindy Ventrice, and Marcia Yudkin.

Contents

Foreword by Susan RoAne   17

Introduction   21

Chapter 1   25

     How to Develop Your News Hook and Become a Media Darling

Chapter 2   51

     How to Get Interviewed by the Print Media

Chapter 3   61

     How to Reach Your Target Audience Through Radio Interviews

Chapter 4   75

     How to Create Celebrity Status via Television Interviews

Chapter 5   97

     How to Media Train Yourself

Chapter 6   115

     Creative Networking and Marketing Techniques to Build Buzz

Chapter 7   133

    How Writing a Book can Build Buzz, Brand, and Business

Chapter 8   165

    How to Build Buzz With Public Speaking

Chapter 9   195

    Creating Buzz for Your Business Through Articles

Chapter 10   213

    Building Buzz, Brand, and Business Through Online Promotion

Resources and Recommended Reading   243

Index   247

About the Author   253

When people learn that I used to be a public school teacher, they often ask me how I got to where I am now: best-selling author, keynote speaker, and the recognized networking authority often quoted in both respected and very unlikely tomes. Believe me, it's a tale that took place over the course of 25 years and it was inauspiciously precipitated by one of the first major layoffs of tenured teachers in the country. And the process is one that increased my GHQ...grey hair quotient. Thank goodness there are cover-ups (legal, of course) for that problem.

What I do know is that if I had Marisa D'Vari's book in my hands then...as you have it in your hands now...the process would have been much easier, less time consuming, and far less stressful. Yes, I built buzz using most of the recommendations put forth in this wonderful book, but if I had this concise, practical, and easy-to-follow guide then, the buzz would not only have been in a shorter time frame, but also in a more logical, organized manner and with a greater feeling of control on my part.

Anyone who has a business, a product, a service, or a career will benefit from buying and, even more importantly, *reading* this book. I recommend having a yellow highlighter in hand and a pad of paper at your side for the "notes to self" you will want to capture. Those notes will be the first draft of your buzz building plan. This is not a book to be skimmed; it is one to read very carefully as you think about your goals, product, expertise, and experiences.

So much of the buzz I have created comes from the conversations I have had over the years with friends, colleagues, and, even more importantly, with strangers. So much in life comes to those who will talk to people they don't know...even in strange places. Eight years ago, I noticed Marisa in a ladies room at a Chicago hotel where we attended a conference. She was also wearing a very stylish St. John outfit, so it seemed natural to make a comment and compliment her because we had something in common. Her response, and our conversation and sharing of information, has had a long-lasting result, which is why you are reading my introduction to her book. Because of that conversation, Marisa became active in the National Speakers Association and was a columnist for *Professional Speaker* magazine. That is the way the world works when we understand that being open leads to unplanned, but very positive results.

I encourage you to pay attention to Chapter 6 to understand the difference between the ability to work a room and the skills involved in networking. In *The Secrets of Savvy Networking*, I first revealed the three tenets of networking, and the one we need to bear in mind on a daily basis is that networking is *not* a spreadsheet activity. Marisa provides a solid reminder: It is not about sales; it is about relationships, being connected to others, and staying in touch so that your market and your contacts remember you.

When my first book, *How to Work a Room*, was published, an attendee at one of my speeches asked me to define the concept. I thought a minute, and said, "It's what you do when no one left you an inheritance for the advertising budget." *Building Buzz* is what you will want to read to be sure that you have a source, a guide, a game plan to reach, impress, and connect with your target audience if you don't have megabucks for advertising.

From writing press releases, to writing articles, to getting booked on the media, to utilizing the Internet as part of your promotion package, Marisa D'Vari offers the entire banquet of buzz and business-building strategies, as well as how to implement them. Trust me…these strategies work.

—Susan RoAne

Susan RoAne, aka "The Mingling Maven," is a keynote speaker, best-selling author of *How to Work a Room* and the new *How to Create Your Own Luck: The "You Never Know" Approach to Networking, Taking Chances, and Opening Yourself to Opportunity*, and is the nation's undisputed and original networking authority (*www.susanroane.com*).

Introduction

Have you ever felt a flash of envy when you saw a competitor—or a colleague—grinning up at you from the pages of your local paper?

You are right to be jealous—the media can crown you as an expert and can give you the all-important third-party credibility that positions you as the expert of choice and elevates you above your competition.

While mastering the secrets of getting media attention is a large part of building buzz for your business, the overall focus of this book is to show you the myriad of ways you can reach out and connect with your target audience for name recognition, elevated status, and additional revenue.

Building buzz is the art of creating awareness and spreading positive word of mouth about the value you provide to clients and customers. It is a way to highlight your expertise and tightly position yourself in your niche. Far from blatant self-promotion, the building buzz techniques described in this book will help you develop a positive image and top of the mind awareness for your product or service among your targeted clients and customers.

Position Yourself for Success

Wardrobe consultant Mary Lou Andre had faith success would be hers, even when she was so broke she had to sell her wedding dress for money to start her wardrobe consulting business. Andre snared a CNN television interview simply by sending fashion correspondent Elsa Klensch her print newsletter, paving the way for national recognition, corporate-sponsored speaking events, and the book *Ready to Wear: An Expert's Guide to Choosing and Using Your Wardrobe*.

Greg Godek, a former teacher at the Cambridge Adult Center and author of the originally self-published *1001 Ways to Be Romantic*, ultimately amassed more than 2 million in book sales following his appearance on *Oprah* and other shows.

Nancy Michaels was able to rise above the myriad of other marketing specialists via her syndicated columns in major business magazines, media appearances, strategic networking, and the latest of her four books, *Perfecting Your Pitch: 10 Proven Strategies for Winning the Clients Everyone Wants* (Career Press, 2005).

Andre, Godek, and Michaels are just a few of the "everyday people" you'll meet who were able to turn their dreams into reality and build buzz for their businesses by tapping into the power of the free media and the many techniques you will read about in this book.

Building Your Platform

A half-century ago, simply attending an Ivy League school put you firmly on the yellow brick road to success. Today, people in the position to hire or recommend you look to your platform—your body of accomplishments—before they decide to do business with you.

Wolfgang Puck has a platform. Three decades ago, he was simply a chef who established a niche with designer pizza. Savvy networking and media appearances launched him to celebrity status, giving him the kind of national platform that makes any business venture he desires possible.

This book is designed to help you establish the kind of national platform that will result in exciting new opportunities and ventures.

Why is a national platform important?

A New York literary agent interviewed for this book boldly declared she only accepts queries from non-fiction authors with a strong national platform, her tone suggesting she couldn't be bothered with anyone else. Unfortunately, she is not alone.

Regardless of whether you are an author, businessperson, or other professional, to be successful you need to begin now to build a platform that establishes you as the expert of choice in your industry or your niche.

The good news is that you already have everything you need to develop your platform, which is the wealth of information and experience stored in your brain and in the raw data contained in your file cabinets and computer folders. In the course of the pages to come, you will learn how to transform this information into articles, booklets, books, public talks, and quotes in the media.

The Power of Belief

When actor Jim Carrey was young and broke, living in a single room with his wife and daughter while honing his craft at a Los Angeles comedy club, he drove to the Hollywood Hills each night and envisioned himself a successful actor. He even wrote himself a 5 million dollar check, with an inner knowingness within that it would soon become a reality.

If the mind can conceive it, then you can achieve it.

Make this your mantra. Success happened for Carrey, and it happened for dozens of other people you will read about in this book. Yet you must have 100 percent faith that success, however you envision it, will be yours.

Visualization is a huge component of achievement. See yourself in a positive light, confidently and firmly working towards establishing a name and presence as the leading expert in your field, and then e-mail me at Success@BuildingBuzz.com to share your success!

1

How to Develop Your News Hook and Become a Media Darling

To have a great idea, have a lot of them.
—Thomas A. Edison,
American Inventor
(1847–1931)

Getting your name in media is the best way to attract your target market. When prospects, clients, and colleagues see you on television or read about you in top national and city newspapers, you develop cache, celebrity status, and take the first steps in developing the kind of national platform that establishes you as the "go-to" expert in your field.

As publicity paves the way for serendipitous positive outcomes, you will soon find yourself an in-demand media darling whose appearances pave the way for speaking engagements, bylined articles, and book deals.

Eileen Roth, a professional organizer just a year into her business, was able to use techniques outlined in this chapter to book herself on the *Today* show and *The Oprah Winfrey Show*, which led to a book deal with a major publisher and catapulted her above her competitors.

Her secret?

 Understanding the importance of a strong news hook.

Understanding the News Hook

It's natural to assume that the print and broadcast media will want to interview you simply because you are an expert in your field. The truth is, you have to earn their interest by providing them with the kind of news hook that shows:

> ❭ You understand what their audience values.

> ❭ You have tied what you want to promote into what's going on in the world today.

> ❭ You have read, watched, or listened to that specific media outlet and know how you would fit in.

In short, before you approach a media outlet, you have to brainstorm why your news is relevant and of high interest to their audience. This is your "pitch," which can be given as a verbal pitch, an e-mail/fax pitch, or can form the basis of a format-specific document called the news release (also known as the media release or press release).

Story Ideas: Where Free Publicity Begins

The media demands "new news." If your story could have been told last week, or next week, they are not interested. Relevance and timeliness are essential to any media outlet.

Your news must whet the appetite and imagination of the editor, reporter, or producer so he can visualize the compelling *story* at the nucleus of your pitch. He needs to see at a glance how your news will play out on paper, radio, or TV, and how your news will appeal to the needs and interests of his readers.

This means you must first find relevant, newsworthy story ideas and condense them into information-packed, "user-friendly" pitches and releases that will shout "great story" to the media professionals reading them.

How to Find Great Story Ideas

Story ideas are all around you. Media folk are shackled to their desks, but you have a fat Rolodex packed with clients, access to research and insider trade publications, phone calls from clients with cutting-edge questions, fresh visits to niche trade shows, and more.

Begin Your Day Brainstorming With the Daily Paper

Get into the habit of reading your city paper with a notebook and pen in hand. Scan the headlines of each section and ask yourself, *"What is in the news today that ties in with what I want to promote?"*

Assume you are the author of a book about romance. You read a feature story in *USA TODAY* about a new study from a major university that suggests couples who favor one another with small, random acts of kindness enjoy happier and more fulfilling marriages. You can use the announcement of this study as a peg for a pitch or release.

Let's say that you live in Boston and, as an author and local resident, your news would be of interest to the *Boston Globe* or the locally produced television show *Chronicle*.

Let's position our news for the *Globe* first. Having kept a sharp eye on the types of stories the *Globe* lifestyle reporters typically cover, you decide the best candidate is Beth Wang, who prefers her pitches in e-mail form. You create a pitch e-mail that might read something like this:

example

Subject Line: Can a Hershey's Kiss save a marriage?

Beth,

Just today, researchers at Stanford University announced a study suggesting that small, random acts of kindness produce more fulfilling marriages. As the Boston-based author of *Romance Forever*, here are five ideas your readers can use immediately to add spice to their lives:

1. Tuck a love note and Hershey's Kiss into her briefcase.

2. Surprise a spouse with a catered romantic picnic in the park.

3. Get a subscription to her favorite magazine.

4. Buy a plant for his office.

5. Send a romantic card "just because."

With Valentine's Day just a month away, this can help many Boston couples strengthen their marriages. If I can be of service, let me know. The couples I interviewed in my book would be honored to share their stories of how small, romantic acts of kindness improved their lives. I can be reached at (give contact information).

Note the journalist was called by her first name, a tactic used to grab the journalist's attention and make her feel as if she is reading a highly personalized e-mail. Today, with advanced software that inserts a person's first name to make a pitch seem personalized, you can easily automatically "mass e-mail" the same pitch to a variety of targeted media folk.

Now let's see how we would take the same study and create a pitch that would interest George, the producer of the Boston-based TV show *Chronicle*:

Subject Line: Valentine's Day Special: Can a Hershey's Kiss save a marriage?

George,

Just today, researchers at Stanford University announced a study suggesting that small, random acts of kindness produce more fulfilling marriages. Boston-based Tony and Tina Brown were headed toward divorce until they learned the advantages of taking time out from their hectic lives to show in small, daily ways how much they meant to one another.

As the Boston-based author of *Romance Forever*, consider a segment featuring the Browns (who were interviewed for my book) sharing the secrets of success with your audience and myself providing expert commentary on how couples can perform small, daily acts of kindness. Tips are detailed below:

1. Tuck a love note and Hershey's Kiss into her briefcase.

2. Surprise a spouse with a catered romantic picnic in the park.

3. Get a subscription to her favorite magazine.

4. Buy a plant for his office.

5. Send a romantic card "just because."

   With Valentine's Day just a month away, this can help many Boston couples strengthen their marriages. You can find my bio and more tips on my Website (give Web address), and I can be reached at (give contact information).

In the *Chronicle* pitch, the producer would likely view the tips as "visuals" he could televise while the voices of the Browns and the expert are heard in the background.

What elevates this pitch above mere piggybacking on a case study is that it incorporates a variety of *additional* positioning techniques you will read about in this section, including tying the book in with a holiday and constructing it in a tip-related format.

The Tip Sheet

The previous pitches also serve as an example of a very popular form of release called the tip sheet. When you create a tip sheet style release, it's easy for an editor, radio show host, or TV news announcer to cut and paste the tips (with your permission) into "filler" material, crediting you with the information and mentioning your book, service, or product.

During the dark days immediately following 9/11, exercise guru Richard Simmons sent out a tip sheet style release with a headline suggesting that in times of national crisis, Americans tend to overeat, listing five tips on how to eat in moderation. The release got picked up by several national and cable news stations whose anchors read it on the air.

Both talk show and music radio hosts often include quick, quirky tips to amuse their listeners or fill time.

Newspapers and magazines make use of tips most often. Newspapers sometimes find themselves with space to fill if an advertisement gets pulled at the last moment, while magazines use tips in the "front of the book" section, which features short, 250-word articles. Editors appreciate tips in the form of a release because it fills the "front of the book" section and they don't have to pay a writer.

As you can see, the tip sheet style release is easy to construct and holds solid information, not fluff. Just write five tips about your subject of expertise, framed in a way your audience will find useful.

Tip sheet style releases are particularly effective for motivating people to send away for free information or a low-cost item. Authors of books and booklets find the tip sheet format quite useful in publicizing their work and generating sales. Marketing guru Marcia Yudkin sent a tip sheet style release with a booklet offer to a variety of publications, resulting in a volume of sales and ultimately forming the basis of her Career Press book, *6 Steps to Free Publicity.* Author Bob Bly also had success with the tip sheet format, which resulted in 3,500 orders for a booklet priced at $7 each.

Take Advantage of a Media Frenzy Surrounding a Juicy Scandal

Janet Jackson got millions of dollars of free publicity resulting from her stunt during the Super Bowl. When a big scandal breaks, the media pounces on it and suddenly the world can't stop watching the pictures and interviews on the TV news. News reporters scramble to dig up related stories, knowing the appetite of their insatiable readers.

And savvy media magicians know that it's fair game to exploit the now famous victim, to hitchhike onto their media bandwagon.

Stanford law professor and former SEC Commissioner Joseph Grundfest is one such individual. Grundfest oversees the Stanford Securities Class Action Clearinghouse and was interviewed by *Fortune* magazine (August 11, 2003) to speak on securities class action litigation.

When asked to give a two-word explanation for the corporate scandals in recent years, Grundfest said, "Winona Ryder," referring to the much-publicized shoplifting scandal surrounding the actress.

As Grundfest explains in the *Fortune* interview, "If you look at Winona Ryder, she knew when the cashmere went into the bag and the bag went out the door that she was violating laws that have been on the books for a very long time. So why did she do it? She figured the probability of getting caught was low…and that nothing terrible would happen (if she did). It's highly likely that a very large percentage of the executives who committed wrongs engaged in exactly the same calculus."

Grundfest took the same approach with Martha Stewart when he said that "…Martha may be guilty of crimes of upholstery. Not only is she alleged to have engaged in a cover-up, but it was a chintzy and tasteless cover-up."

Read Financial Indices Daily

Every single day, statistics change. This is news. Stocks go up or down. Interest rates fluctuate or "threaten to fluctuate," which can inspire thousands of hours of debate on TV and millions of pounds of newspaper ink.

Whatever you wish to promote can be tied into the financial indices. Along with your freshly brewed coffee, get into the habit of perusing fluctuating financial data as a way of coming up with a story angle that hooks into your industry. Even a fashion designer can use the rise or fall of interest rates to comment on this season's hemlines (a time-honored publicity tool dating from the 1927 crash). Regardless of what you want to promote, there is a way for you to tie it in with financial statistics.

Why is financial data so powerful?

Consider interest rates. Because a home is the primary source of wealth for the majority of Americans, anything that threatens this investment is big news.

Let's assume you are a real estate agent or mortgage broker, and you want to get more clients as buyers and sellers. When interest rates nudge up, people are concerned, wondering if the boom is over. If you can create a sensational headline with solid information or tips on how folks can decide whether to buy, sell, or hold, you have an excellent chance of placement.

Surveys Can Inspire Solid Story Ideas

In the course of working within your core industry, you come across a multitude of surveys in trade publications or in client research. You can piggyback on these surveys to generate new story ideas with great success.

Why do the media salivate when they see a reference to a survey? It comes down to three key reasons:

1. The media views quantitative data as more accurate.

2. Surveys can be turned into graphs and charts that have an eye-stopping "visual" appeal to print along with the column.

3. You are shedding new, quantitative light on a hot, happening topic.

Listen to Questions Your Clients & Customers Ask You

Are you suddenly hearing people asking you the same question? If you are in the financial markets, it may be, "Is it time to get back into stocks?" If you are a diet coach, it may be, "Is it time to consider essential amino acids instead of conventional diet pills?" If clients and customers are suddenly asking you the same questions, it means buzz is building around this topic—and it's time for you to turn it into a story idea!

Read Trade Publications for Industry Trends

Because you have established a niche in your industry, you are more focused than most journalists in breaking developments. What is the buzz in your trade publications? What are new developments in your field? Because you have access to all this information, you can spot developments sooner than journalists and establish yourself as an expert source.

Find Story Ideas in the Course of Your Daily Routine

Perfect strangers can inspire great story ideas journalists will love. If you are in financial services, listen up when perfect strangers ask for advice or open up about their financial habits. At the Sports Club LA, a 23-year-old male physical trainer told me that he'd been socking away money in his IRA since he was 16. Now if you were a financial planner, what a great anecdote this would be to pique the interest of a reporter, who could use this as the lead of his article and follow with your tips on planning for retirement.

Listen to Comedians on Cable and Late Night Talk Shows for Inspiration

Comedians and late night talk show hosts (or their writers) have their fingers on the pulse of the universal trends everyone is talking about. You can use their topics for "outside-of- the-box thinking" on your own subjects to give them a new spin, or simply file away their subjects and stories for anecdotes.

When mainstream comedians cite trends or people, use the same trends or people in your talks, queries, articles, and headlines. These individuals (such as Martha Stewart) and their all-too-human foibles become "universal symbols" of the concepts you are trying to get across.

Give Evergreen Stories Topical New Twists

Have you noticed that weight-loss articles fill newspapers and magazines every January? In February, every article seems to center on romance. Issues of April magazines are flooded with stories on saving taxes.

Editors have a pressing need for evergreen stories but prefer a fresh twist. Consider your topic of expertise and how you can tie it in with a seasonal occurrence or holiday to use as a news peg for your own news.

Working With Holidays

Most people assume that the only real holidays are the season favorites of New Year's Eve, Valentine's Day, etc. But the truth is anyone can create their own holiday in three ways. You can go to city hall and get the mayor to agree to a signed proclamation for a specific day. You can read John Kremer's *Celebrate Today* or visit *www.BookMarket.com* for directions on how to create a holiday. Or, you can visit the reference desk at your local library and flip to the back page of *Chase's Calendar of Events* and fill out the form to create a holiday with a special meaning to you.

Why do people create holidays? Mostly to draw publicity to their business or a cherished cause. To honor my cat and give homage to cats throughout the world, I created Hug Your Cat Day for *Chase's Calendar of Events*. As creator, I do not "own" the holiday; others are welcome to piggyback on it (i.e. using it as a news peg to promote their own agenda). Franklin Covey, for example, include this holiday in many of their calendars. (See page 37.)

Two savvy radio DJs in San Francisco, both named Kat, decided to use my holiday as a springboard for their own "Hug Your Cat Day," in which they took hugs from fans so as to raise visibility for their respective radio stations and raise much-needed funds for the MSPCA.

Timing Your Holiday

Hug Your Cat Day is a holiday created to fall on the first day of Book Expo America (BEA). The reason is that the book *Apricat Does the Ritz* will have its launch date at BEA, and celebrating this holiday in the thick of the media frenzy will go a long way towards ensuring its success.

I GOTTA BUY SOME
LIGHTER UNDERWEAR

THURSDAY 13	FRIDAY 14	SATURDAY 15
		Hug Your Cat Day

8

9

10

11

12

1

		SUNDAY 16
		National Nothing Day

2

3

4

5

6

7
8

Today's Chores	Today's Chores	Today's Chores

National Clean Off Your Desk Day takes place in January because this is the month most people try to keep their New Year's resolution of a clean and orderly desk.

Creating a holiday is free. Simply fill out the form at the back of *Chase's Calendar of Events* and send it in. As creator, you have your contact information listed in the directory itself, so the media will call and interview you for more information.

Because it takes nearly two years to get listed in the next annual edition of this directory, you might wonder how you can use it as a promotional tool this very day as a news peg. The answer is simply to piggyback on existing holidays to use them to promote your own services in both print and TV/radio.

The News Release

Your goal is to hook the media's interest with tempting bait. Traditionally, this was accomplished with the news release (also called a press release and media release), a specifically formatted document with a strong headline giving the *who*, *what*, *why*, *when*, *where*, and *how* of a story.

In the days before faxes and e-mail, people gave more attention to mailed news releases. But today, with the advent of distribution services that mass fax and mass e-mail releases at low prices, media folk are overwhelmed with untargeted information and find that the majority of releases are:

> Dull and boring.

> Failing to get to the point.

> Failing to establish relevance to the publication or show.

> ❭ Failing to establish relevance to the media outlet's audience.

> ❭ Not timely.

The basic form of a news release is a single page of double-spaced information. Your contact information should be in the top left, and the words "for immediate release" should be used unless you want to "embargo" the news until a certain date, as would be the case if you want all types of media to release the news at the same time.

At the end of the release, type and center the pound sign three times (###) to signal your release has ended and there are no additional pages.

Print News Release on the Internet

Is there a difference between a traditional print or faxed release and one that is posted on the Internet? In a word, *yes*.

The form may look identical, but the secret of writing an effective news release to be posted on the Web is using the right keywords.

I will discuss online publicity at length in the chapter devoted to this subject, but the key point to remember here is that the online, Internet-based release will come up in a search engine when a user types in specific keywords. So before you begin to write your news release for the Internet, make a long list of all the keywords a journalist or other person could possibly use if they were trying to get information on the kind of product or service you offer. Then, artfully weave those keywords into the body of your news release, paying more attention to using them closer to the top of your release.

Choosing Between a Faxed or Mailed News Release and an E-mail Pitch

When you hunt down contact information for media folk using media directories found in the public library, you will notice a field called "preferences." In this field, media folk state their preference to be contacted by e-mail, fax, or mail. To ignore a preference is to risk the media person not seeing your release at all.

In a 1997 survey, Thomas Rankin Associates asked trade editors how they preferred to receive releases.

The answers:

> ❯ By mail: 94 percent.

> ❯ By fax: 2 percent.

> ❯ By e-mail: 0.

By 1999, Rankin found 88 percent of editors welcomed e-mailed releases. After the 9/11 terrorist attacks and anthrax scare, snail mail was tested for bioterrorism at most major media outlets, further enhancing the media's embrace of information via e-mail.

Trust, but Verify

A media person's preference for receiving e-mail or faxed information can change at a moment's notice. At a Publicity Club meeting in New England, Geoff Eggers, a journalist for the "Living Arts" section of the *Boston Globe*, reported he gets a lot of misplaced pitches and news releases that do not pertain to his exclusive beat of architecture and museums.

Journalists and producers can get hundreds of pitches a day. When you take the time to make sure your information is targeted to their beat or area of interest and hone your pitch to their publication or show, you gain respect and take the first steps in building a long relationship. If you spam them with pitches unrelated to their niche, they will learn to delete your e-mails or faxes as they pop up or, worse, put you on their block list, which filters out your e-mails before they reach the inbox.

Rather than risk a perfectly tailored news release never reaching the media person you are targeting, make a 15-second call to ask two key questions:

1. Are you the appropriate person to receive a news release on this topic? If not, who is?

2. Do you prefer your releases sent by fax or e-mail? (Make sure to verify the number and address.)

Print (or Faxed) News Release vs. E-mail Pitch

The difference between sending a fax and an e-mail is that the e-mail pitch must be as tightly focused, snappy, and eye-catching as a one-page print release, but deliver all that information and even more motivating text in the preview window of a typical e-mail inbox, which in preview mode is about the first three lines.

Here are key points to remember:

❯ Subject lines are of prime importance.

❯ Use a strong headline in bolded text as your first line.

> Underscore the headline with a subheading (in italics).

> Keep your e-mail to three short paragraphs, with no paragraph more than three lines for easy scanning.

> Include a link where the media can find a longer release or more information on your Website.

Do's and Don'ts of E-mail Pitching

> Keep the tone of your e-mail friendly and conversational, as if you were writing to a friend.

> Bulleted points make for easy scanning.

> Include links to relevant areas of your Website in addition to your phone number.

> If you mail merge the release, be very cautious about making sure others are hidden in the bcc (blind copy) field of your e-mail.

> Send yourself a test message to check the format of the e-mail.

> Never send an attachment. Train yourself to use Internet links for everything.

> Avoid words in both the subject line and text that could get you banned by spam filters. After you self-check, perform a final test with a spam checker. (For the latest free spam checkers, conduct an Internet search using the keywords "spam checker.")

> Be certain your contact information is in the body of the e-mail release.

Universal Elements of a Release Sent by Mail, Fax, and E-mail

In the following sections, you will learn how to write a compelling news release. If you are going to be sending this release by e-mail, understand that the subject line and the first three sentences determine if your e-mail gets read at all—so make sure it's as compelling, relevant, and timely as possible.

In All Releases, Headlines Are Key

The most important element of your release is the ability of your headline to catch the reporter's eye. In fact, in the days of mass faxing, many reporters would roll the release up in a ball as it popped out of the machine. The only thing that would stop them, mid crumple, was an arresting headline.

What makes a headline arresting?

Once again, the twin virtues of *relevance* and *timeliness* combined with a strong benefit and a witty, eye-catching spin.

According to advertising expert David Ogilvy, headlines are the most important element of your release because more than 90 percent of people glance at the headline without reading anything more.

So, what are the elements of an effective headline?

You have actually seen them if you ever waited in line at a grocery store and had been tempted by the bank of colorful magazines with cover headlines suggesting "7 Ways to Lose Weight by Friday" and "6 Tips to Spot a Cheating Husband."

The best headlines have numbers to catch the eye (there is a reason Moses brought back the 10 Commandments and why Stephen R. Covey found a best-seller in *The 7 Habits of Highly Effective People*) and offer immediate gratification in the form of a clear benefit for reading the text.

Media folk are busy, with most admitting to giving the headline (or subject line of an e-mail) a half-second glance before tossing or deleting a release. In the headline, media people scan for:

> ❯ Relevance to their beat or segment.

> ❯ Relevance to their publication or show.

> ❯ A new trend or twist on a classic or evergreen story.

> ❯ A topic currently of heated interest in the news.

> ❯ A story that would offer a strong benefit to their highly targeted audience.

Keeping these points in mind, tweak your headline until you are certain it will grab the media person's eye and motivate her to read the first line of text. Some tried and true headline formats include beginning with "5 Tips to _____," asking a question, or crafting a "how to" headline that would solve a problem for the publication's target audience.

Easy Ways to Construct Headlines That Get Read

1. Lead with a number, followed by the word "tips" or "ways" to do XYZ.

2. Begin with a number, followed by the phrase "mistakes most often made" in XYZ.

3. Feature a strong benefit in your headline.

4. Address a problem and provide a solution in the sub-headline.

5. Create a stronger "how to" headline by following up with words like "get," "avoid," "start," "become," "have," "begin," "stop," "end," and "enjoy."

Summary Blurb & Sub-Headlines

Attention spans are short. Instead of reading all the paragraphs of your release or pitch, a summary blurb or sub-headline fits the needs of today's information-dazed media folk who need to "skim" a crisp, descriptive sentence or short summary paragraph before deciding whether to invest the time in reading the entire release or pitch. It should be short and punchy, much like the one-line TV guide description of a movie.

This summary blurb and sub-headline should:

❯ Be 13 words or less (remember, keep it simple and straightforward).

❯ Use fresh, descriptive words that underscore relevance.

❯ Not repeat words from your headline.

Special Subject/Headline Needs of E-mail Releases

Because your e-mail subject line should only hold five exciting, tantalizing words, you'll want to spend serious time thinking about what would motivate the media person to open it.

Your actual release headline follows in the e-mail plain text body.

The Release/Pitch Body

Continuing on the theme that attention spans are short and journalists are looking for any excuse to delete your release/pitch and move on, creating a compelling first line in your release/pitch body is essential. Train yourself to write in an inverted pyramid style so the most compelling, relevant, and timely information is at the top. Support your timely, relevant, compelling first sentence with quotes, facts, statistics, or anecdotes that support it from credible sources.

Re-read your release from the point of view of a time-crunched media person who is asking himself the following questions as he skims the release:

> ❯ How is this information relevant to my column, show segment, and/or target audience?

> ❯ How can this information help my readers, listeners, or viewers solve a key problem?

> ❯ Does the information in this release suggest a growing trend or concern?

> ❯ Why does my audience need to know this information as quickly as possible?

The secret to writing effective releases and pitches is finding newsworthy story ideas that are direct links between what you want to promote and what audiences of your target media outlets yearn to learn more about.

Follow Up With a Phone Script

Check most of the preferences in the media directories and you will find that the majority of reporters, editors, and producers discourage follow-up calls. If you are confident you correctly targeted the appropriate media person with relevant, timely information, go ahead and call.

But spend some time creatively thinking of a new, fresh angle other than, "Did you get my news release or story idea?"

Brainstorm and shape new information on the subject of your initial e-mail and *stress another reason* why your news needs to printed or broadcast as soon as possible.

Before you dial, work out a script for what you are going to say. *Practice it.* Then keep calling until you can get the media person live. If voice mail seems to be your only option, leave a voice message that sounds something like this:

"John Smith here, 212-555-5555. Last week I sent you my story idea for XYZ, but there's *breaking news* in this subject I want you to know about. Again, John Smith, 212-555-5555."

Now you are not *bothering* the media person; you are offering "new news" on a topic that relates to his niche and target audience.

Getting Contact Information for the Media

You can get contact information for the media in four key ways:

1. **Using media directories such as Bacon's, Burrelle's, Gebbie Press, and Gale's, which are available at most libraries.**

If you elect to use the library to get contact information, call the reference desk to make sure that particular branch has the latest edition of the media directories. In Boston, for example, the Kirstein Business Library has a more updated version than the Boston Public Library.

Bring a roll of dimes to photocopy individual pages of the directories or bring a laptop computer to create your own media database on the spot. As even "new" media directories go out of date almost as soon as they are printed, call the media outlet to verify all information.

2. **Buying your own online directory. (See "Resources and Recommended Reading.")**

Investing in your own online directory is the easiest method of getting media attention. Yet although online databases are updated regularly, it's still necessary to call and verify key contacts are still employed.

3. **Creating your own database by entering the contact information of media people you read, watch, or listen to on a regular basis.**

Entering contacts into your media database as you come across them in your daily reading, listening, and viewing life is a great way to get started, as you are already familiar with these outlets and have predetermined they are right for the news you want to present.

4. **Using a search engine on the Internet to find newspapers, radio stations, TV shows, and related contact information.**

For example, entering phrases into a search engine such as "talk radio stations" and "national" can yield great results. Try various search engines and arrangements of words.

Sorting Your Media Contacts

Every pitch or release you send out should be highly targeted to specific media folk who are a good fit for your news.

Sometimes you will have several candidates. Because you must make follow-up calls to all, make this a doable task by dividing your list into three segments.

Your A-list are your most desirable contacts, the media outlets that will reach your target market or are so prestigious or popular they will look good listed on your Website and collateral material.

Your B-list are smaller publications that lack glamour, such as a trade publication, but are read by colleagues and clients.

Your C-list includes all the rest.

If you are just getting started, begin making follow-up calls with your B-list as practice. If you face rejection (for example, they covered the topic before), see if you can give it a new twist. Take any feedback or insights, tweak your pitch, and call the A-list.

In theory, most media outlets don't want to cover a subject if it's been covered by another outlet. But sometimes, outlets in your C-list will be impressed if you got coverage for your topic in a top publication and may see your news as a trend. So call your C-list, tell them of your media placements, and there's a good chance they will pick it up.

Chapter Summary

1. Identify your target audience.

2. Focus on a news hook.

3. Develop a sixth sense for timely, appropriate story ideas.

4. Use the daily paper and its headlines for inspiration.

5. Consider evergreen stories with a twist.

6. Read financial indices and find a creative way to tie this ever-changing, headline-generating field into what you want to promote.

7. Consider surveys, especially when co-authored with an educational institution, to give what you want to promote a hard news slant.

8. Listen to questions asked by your clients and customers to generate ideas for releases and direct pitches.

9. An attention-getting headline is crucial in getting your release read.

10. Tips and lists with a strong news angle make for content-rich releases that get read.

Chapter Assignments

☐ Carry a notebook and jot down names of media folk who cover your beat for your media database.

☐ Create and refine a series of running story ideas.

☐ Take one story idea and position it to suit the demographics of a particular media outlet.

☐ Before sending your story idea off to a media contact, verify by phone he is the appropriate person to receive the news and double-check his preferred method of receiving information.

☐ Create a follow-up script that offers breaking news, or a new twist, on the subject that heightens the reasons the story needs to be told *now*.

2

How to Get Interviewed by the Print Media

> *Glory is fleeting,*
> *but obscurity is forever.*
> —Napoleon Bonaparte,
> Military Leader (1769–1821)

Imagine how thrilling it would be to open up the *Wall Street Journal* and see your business written up in glowing terms by a prestigious reporter. Even better, realize how mainstream media coverage would elevate your prestige in the minds of your clients.

This happened to Diane Darling, author of *The Networking Survival Guide*, when an announcement she sent for one of her workshops grabbed the attention of a *WSJ* reporter. Julie Michaud, owner of Michaud Cosmetics, is routinely written up in the glossy consumer magazines *In Style* and *Allure*, and in various local and bridal publications. Each month, skin care specialist Nance Mitchell's name pops up in glossy magazines around the globe.

These small business owners did not use a publicist; instead, they mastered the art of positioning themselves to the media as an expert source in their niche.

When prospective clients read about you in a newspaper, magazine, or trade publication, they look upon you with new respect. Psychologically, it's as if the publication is signaling you out and positioning you *above* your competitors.

In this chapter, we will explore low- and no-cost ways of building buzz about your business. The steps consist of:

1. Discovering publications read by your target audience.

2. Reading these publications to get a feel for their content.

3. Getting contact information for journalists.

4. Offering yourself as an expert source to journalists.

What Does Your Target Market Read?

Your first step is to spend serious time defining your target market. Who are they? Create a mental picture of them in your mind. Next, ask yourself the kind of publications they read. Take out your notebook and make a broad list. The basics of your list can consist of:

> Your city paper.

> Your city's business journal.

> Neighborhood papers.

> National papers (such as the *Wall Street Journal, USA TODAY,* and the *New York Times*).

❭ Trade publications.

❭ Association publications and newsletters.

❭ Consumer business publications.

❭ General consumer publications.

In addition, consider what "influencers" read. An influencer is someone such as a human resources executive or accountant who helps the buyer make hiring decisions or someone who is in the position to pass on referrals.

Using Pitchcraft

To interest a reporter in your story, you must use pitchcraft. This does not involve a magical spell, but it does require that you not only read the publication, but study it to ensure you strategize your pitch correctly.

The No. 1 complaint of editors is that people pitch them without understanding what kind of news they are looking for. *Ladies' Home Journal* and *Good Housekeeping* may look the same to you, but to the editors, the differences are night and day.

You may also think that you can send the same pitch to a business reporter at the *Boston Globe* and the *Boston Herald*. Though both papers may be able to use your news, you would need to angle the pitch differently.

Study the publications your target audience reads in order to gain an understanding of:

❭ The type of stories they typically cover.

❭ The type of experts they usually quote and feature.

> ❯ The section of the newspaper, journal, or magazine most likely to feature you.

> ❯ The beat reporter most likely to be interested in interviewing you.

Finding Contact Information

Let's imagine you are a nutritionist with a theory about safe weight loss. You will want to approach the health or lifestyle beat reporter at a newspaper or a specific columnist at a magazine.

To find this kind of contact information, you decide to flip through the media directories at the library and you see that Stephanie Dolgoff oversees the health and nutrition department for *Self* magazine and that Scott Allen oversees health and science coverage for the *Boston Globe*. You would make note of their contact information and pitch them as you learned in Chapter 1.

Contacting Beat Reporters

Beat reporters have a specific, narrow focus and strive to bring value to their readers. The more you study the beat reporter's articles and objectives, the more success you will have in crafting story ideas for which she will interview you.

It's a good idea to meet reporters who cover your niche in person, but most reporters today are overworked and have little time. If you are trying to meet beat reporters in your city, consider joining your area's publicity club. Most cities have them, and you don't have to be a member to attend the monthly gatherings, which feature informative panel discussions with journalists.

For example, at the Publicity Club of New England (found via the Internet by entering the words "publicity club" plus "Boston" in the Google search engine), one can learn many insider secrets from panels consisting of business editors, healthcare reporters, TV assignment desk editors, and more. It's a great way for an expert to meet reporters who cover his niche.

Offering Yourself as a Source to Journalists

Journalists like to feature several experts in any one article to provide color and a balanced point of view. Recently, CNNmoney.com featured an article about the stock market titled: "Is It Safe to Get Back In?—5 Experts on What to Do Now."

Now, if *you* were a financial expert, wouldn't you want to be one of the five experts quoted so you could enhance your expert status and attract clients?

Author Tina Tessina, a licensed psychotherapist in Southern California, offers herself as a source regularly and, as a result, gets four to five print/TV/radio interviews a week, numerous mentions as an expert in monthly magazines, and has used the buzz to become a host on a weekly radio show, which gives her even more exposure.

Journalists find experts in a variety of ways, but try turning the tables and introduce yourself to an expert first.

Here's the two-step method:

1. Track journalists who write about your niche and feature many experts (as anecdotes) in each article. Put them in your media database.

2. Write them a short, punchy introductory e-mail. The subject line is crucial. The safest way to get your e-mail opened is to comment on a previous article they wrote, such as "feedback on your XYZ article."

Get to the point in the first line of your e-mail. Say you enjoyed his XYZ article and have noticed he writes primarily in the ABC field. Explain the nature of your expertise (briefly) and say should he want expert advice in the future, you are glad to assist.

Instead of an attachment, provide a link to your bio on your Website, as well as a link to other pages in your Website press room (discussed in Chapter 10) you feel are relevant.

If the journalist is a staff member of a publication, feel free to say you will follow up by phone on a specific date. Try calling until you get the journalist live, or else leave a short, punchy voice message.

To get the inside scoop from journalists on how they wish to be contacted by experts, I contacted three top journalists from the prestigious American Society of Journalists and Authors (ASJA): Sam Greengard, Kathy Sena, and Robert McGarvey—all freelancers who write for a variety of publications, but usually center on a niche such as business, health, and technology.

Here is a combination of their advice:

1. Send an e-mail with a clear subject line.

2. Do not send attachments.

3. Include links in the body of your e-mail that lead to Web pages that underscore your expertise.

4. Provide a short bulleted list of story ideas, along with a link leading to information on your expertise.

5. Do not snail mail anything—it will be tossed. Freelance journalists simply don't have the space or mechanism to call up hard print information when needed. With an electronic file, they can let their computer do the searching with keywords.

Sam Greengard mentions that sometimes serendipity works in an expert's favor: "More than once, I'm working on a specific topic and an e-mail pings into my box that is exactly the expert I'm looking for." Increase your chances of serendipity by familiarizing yourself with a journalist and his body of articles, as well as a friendly e-mail with a catchy story idea in the journalist's alley. "One sales consultant caught my eye with his idea that one can't pursue transactions as though they are zero sum game," says McGarvey, who featured him in a story.

Kathy Sena offers solid advice by advising experts to get to the point and be professional, but not have their e-mail be so canned and impersonal it reads like spam.

Mastering Interviews With Journalists

Rushed and on deadline, journalists often pick up the phone and call experts they find in the course of their Internet search, hoping to interview them on the spot. They continue to call experts until they run out of time or surpass their allotted word count. Most experts are often so flattered to receive the call that they answer the journalist's questions then and there.

Wrong move. Even if a journalist is on deadline and you fear he might just call and interview your competition, it's imperative that you have at least seven precious minutes to put your thoughts in order. If your assistant had taken the call, personally tell the journalist you're delighted to talk to him but someone's in your office and you promise to call back in five minutes. Also, ask a bit more about what the story is about and how you can best be of service.

3 Key Message Points

As soon as you hang up the phone, write out three key messages you want to focus on during the interview given the subject matter. Try composing these points in a blank e-mail, which you will ultimately send back to the journalist as written confirmation of your key message points.

In addition to writing the three key points, find ways to support each of the message points through facts, statistics, and anecdotes.

If you are a fast thinker and have natural wit, think of some sound bites that describe what you will be speaking about in a colorful way. Write them down, lest you forget them.

Handling Yourself During the Interview

A phone interview with a journalist is not like radio, where thousands of people are judging you by your words. Still, it is important to keep your energy high, your tone helpful, and be as articulate as possible. Remember that on the other side of the phone line, the journalist is taking fast notes on his computer while at the same time listening to your words and planning the next question. If you want your words to be quoted accurately, speak slowly and, if possible, try to listen for the clicking of computer keys. If you hear the journalist furiously clicking away, pause until you hear him slowing down before finishing your sentence.

What Not to Say to a Reporter

Most reporters are not trying to trip you up, but one characteristic journalists share is the desire to tell a fair and balanced story. At the same time, they know that color and controversy sell. Some journalists might try to put you on the spot with what can be perceived as a hostile question. Others might put you at ease in an attempt to increase the chance you will confide in them.

Resist the temptation to waiver from your three key message points. Avoid saying words like "no comment." Instead, phrase your answer to focus on one of your key points.

Also, resist the temptation to save time or help the journalist out by guessing about a fact or offering information out of your area of expertise. Wrong statistics and incorrect facts can come back to haunt you.

Most important of all, never say anything "off the record." If you vocalized it, it's on the record.

How to Develop a Relationship With a Journalist

The more helpful you are during the interview, the more likely the journalist will use you again as an expert source. You can increase the opportunity of this happening by:

> Asking if they would like to interview other experts and referring them to your association colleagues.

> Asking if you can forward a case study or other documentation that might be of help.

> Sending a thank-you note.

Chapter Summary

1. Understand what your target audience reads and carefully study this publication for clues as to how to shape your message.

2. Pitch beat reporters of newspapers or specific columnists of magazines with news that fits their niche.

3. Before sending any news or release to a journalist, call to verify their "beat" and that they are the appropriate person to send your specific news to. In the same call, verify if they prefer e-mail, fax, phone, or snail mail for their news.

4. Send a journalist an introductory e-mail if you feel you would be a good source of information for them.

5. Do not take a call from a journalist on the spot. Call them back in five minutes so you have time to shape your message.

6. Remember that nothing is ever "off the record."

Chapter Assignments

❑ Begin to carry a notebook and jot down the names of media folk who cover your beat for your media database.

❑ Create and refine a series of running story ideas.

❑ Take one story idea and position it to suit the demographics of a particular media outlet. Pitch the reporter in e-mail form, tying in what you want to promote to the news.

3

How to Reach Your Target Audience Through Radio Interviews

The secret of being tiresome is to tell everything.
—Voltaire, Author and Philosopher (1694–1778)

One of the easiest ways to build buzz for your business is through live radio interviews conducted via telephone from the convenience of your own home or office. Just imagine the value and impact of communicating your message to your target market as they drive, work, or play.

You don't have to be a celebrity to be a talk show radio guest. With more than 10,000 radio stations in the United States alone, producers are looking for lively, informative guests who can edify and entertain their listeners.

Rebecca Morgan, a management consultant in San Jose, California, had been listening to National Public Radio (NPR) when she heard a promotion for a new NPR segment on "Customers From Hell." Because Morgan was an expert on the subject by virtue of having published a successful book titled *Calming Upset Customers*, she called the show's producer and an interview was arranged.

The interview resulted in a plethora of *"I heard you on NPR!"* congratulatory calls from colleagues, clients, and prospects; elevated status; and yet another notch on her long list of media accolades.

Like Morgan, Kimberly McCall, president of McCall Media & Marketing, Inc., was keenly aware that her target market also listened to NPR. She introduced herself to the local Maine producer as an expert source should the need arise and, ultimately, was called to comment on a breaking news story. Her success on that program paved the way for other NPR interviews to come.

Morgan and McCall are both excellent examples of proactively positioning themselves for success by taking the first move in connecting with key radio media. This is as simple as picking up the phone and, like Morgan, speaking with a producer directly when your expertise can assist her in building her show. If Morgan had not offered herself as an expert, the producer would have had to spend many valuable hours finding one. If McCall had never made contact with the NPR producer who ultimately invited her to be an expert guest, that interview and the subsequent interviews that helped brand her and her business would not have happened.

Determine Your "ABC" Radio List

Consider contacting radio producers in accordance with your "ABC" lists, with "A" representing the top markets. In radio, "A" stands for shows your target audience listens to. This can mean NPR or popular syndicated talk shows.

Given your time limitations, consider whether you want to customize your pitch to a specific radio show, or send personalized, albeit mass pitches to several—even hundreds—of stations.

Practice With Call-In Shows

New to radio? Being a call-in guest on radio talk shows allows you to experience what it is like being on the "hot seat" before you are officially recognized as a guest and your clients and colleagues are hearing you speak. You can even use a pseudonym when asked your name.

Try tape-recording your call to see how your voice sounds on the air. Is there hesitancy in your voice? Do you sound confidant and in command?

Confidence—and clear articulation—is crucial. While listening to a syndicated call-in talk show called *The Connection*, I was startled when an author called in to give his opinion on the topic of the day. "Hi," he said by way of introduction to thousands of listeners. "My name is (fast and slurred). And I'm the author of the book (fast and slurred)."

The host asked him what his book was about.

"Well," said the slurring author, "*I guess* it's about...."

If the author does not know what his book is about, *how will anyone else?*

Become a Critic

Begin to listen to radio talk shows on a regular basis. Observe what makes good guests good and bad guests bad. Notice when you suddenly feel like changing the station. When did you begin to mentally "tune them out"?

Did their voice lack *animation*?

By analyzing the interviews of others, you can improve your own performance.

How to Pitch to Radio Producers

Radio producers live in a voice-oriented world.

The voices of radio hosts and DJs live larger than life in the hearts and minds of their core listeners. And the voice of a guest can make a program great or kill it dead.

Therefore, it makes sense to voice a radio producer first with a well-prepared script, whet his appetite for the segment you want to pitch, then send additional material by fax, e-mail, or mail, as he prefers.

To get on radio shows you need:

> ❯ A lively, personable voice.

> ❯ An enticing pitch that piques the interest of the producer on behalf of his station's target audience.

> ❯ Persistence.

When you are on the phone with a producer, use the upbeat, animated voice you would use if you were being interviewed on radio. Remember, this is your *audition*. Also, be ready to fax or e-mail your written pitch and supporting materials immediately. If you fax, be certain every page of your material has your name, number, and Website on it in the event the material becomes separated and the producer needs to contact you. It's also a good idea to have this material available as a link to the media room of your Website (see Chapter 10).

Creating a Pitch for Radio Producers

Consider your message and the type of audience you want to reach. For A-list shows, you will want to listen to programs over several days or weeks, find the most appropriate show(s) where you will be a good fit, find a way to work what you want to promote into "new news," and pitch via the producer's preferred method.

Pitching to A-list radio shows is comparable to pitching to top network morning TV shows. You can get booked, but it requires concentrated effort on your part in terms of matching what the producer values for his audience to the information you want to promote.

Sample E-mail Pitch for Radio

William A. Gordon, author of *The Ultimate Hollywood Tour Book,* prefers to e-mail producers first and follow up by phone a few days later. This technique has allowed him to log more than 400 radio interviews. Following is a sample of a pitch e-mail he sends out, which changes according to celebrity scandals as they hit the news wires:

Did you know that Hugh Hefner paid $125,000 for the privilege of spending eternity next to Marilyn Monroe?

Or that the owners of the *Malcolm in the Middle* house pocketed over $100,000 just by renting their house to the Fox Broadcasting Company?

William A. Gordon, author of *The Ultimate Hollywood Tour Book,* can entertain your listeners with all kinds of anecdotes about Hollywood. He has stories about celebrity homes and haunts; sites where famous motion pictures and TV shows were filmed; infamous Hollywood scandals, murders, and suicides; and all kinds of overlooked attractions (for instance, cemeteries and sites that inspired famous songs).

To schedule an interview, please call Mr. Gordon at (phone number here). Review copies are available on request. We can also provide you with books to give away to listeners.

Sincerely,
Steven Dunn
Director of Marketing
North Ridge Books
Lake Forest, CA

www.nrbooks.com/hollywoodtour.htm

SAMPLE QUESTIONS TO ASK WILLIAM A. GORDON
(phone number here)

1. How much money do people make by renting out their homes to the movies?

2. How did you find out where all these movies and TV shows were filmed? Can you actually see (here you can ask Mr. Gordon about virtually any TV show or movie)?

3. What is "The Flying Saucer" house, and which movies has it appeared in?

The Ultimate Hollywood Tour Book *is available at Barnes & Noble and Amazon.com. Or call toll-free* (toll-free phone number here).

A free sample chapter is online at www.nrbooks.com.

As you can see, Gordon surpassed the three-paragraph rule but says he is successful in immediately hooking the producer with the kind of fun, "gee whiz" facts that grab attention. You will also note that Gordon established his credibility as an author and used the magic words that excite a radio producer's ears:

> *"We can also provide you with books to give away to listeners."*

Listeners love freebies, and producers know that their gratitude goes to the station that made the freebie possible.

Finally, by listing sample questions, the radio producer can get an idea of how the segment would play out. Like most folks who mass e-mail radio stations, Gordon has to be persistent in calling producers back (Gordon likes to do so in the early morning, when they are usually at their desks), as few producers call to book an interview after reading the e-mail.

This approach works well for the general-interest talk shows Gordon is targeting. He has also had success interesting music stations with his pitch. In fact, this approach has worked so well, Gordon now sells his list of contacts for more than 1,100 radio shows that interview guests (see "Resources and Recommended Reading" for contact information).

How to Have Producers Contact You

If you dislike pitching, one option available to you, depending on your area of expertise, is the *Radio-TV Interview Report* (*RTIR*). This trade publication goes to more than 4,000 radio/TV producers across the United States and Canada, and is published three times each month. Each issue lists 100–150 prospective guests (authors and experts) available for live and in-studio interviews. Prospective guests are given a full-, half-, or quarter-page "advertisement" written by top copywriters so their subject sounds enticing and their contact information is available to radio producers.

Debbie Allen, author of *Confessions of Shameless Self Promoters*, has used *RTIR* and claims great success in terms of motivating radio producers to call her for interviews. Her advertisement is shown here.

Over the years, I have spoken with many people about their success with this publication, and the answer is that the more controversial or sensational your message, the more calls you get from radio stations. Typically, radio show producers flip through the pages, looking for a guest to fill an interview spot. (See "Resources and Recommended Reading" for information.)

Shameless Dating Diva Reveals...

How to Find Dates and Hot Mates

Your listeners will laugh out loud and energize their dating skills when **Debbie Allen** — the Shameless Dating Diva — shares everything from how to unleash your inner flirt to ways to meet exciting, attractive people while avoiding "losers."

This veteran dater and author of the new book, *CONFESSIONS OF SHAMELESS DATING*, will delight your audience with her stories and her proven dating tips as she shares:

- How to use a cocktail napkin to find out what you have in common with your date.

- 7 ways to add shameless charm to the first impression you make.

- Where to meet and connect with great singles — and special advice on cyberdating.

- Hilarious tales of dates gone awry and lessons learned from them.

- 10 ways to heal your broken heart and rebuild your self-esteem after a break up.

"Honest, touching and steamy, Debbie Allen's latest book captures our fantasies and runs with them shamelessly all the way to the finish line!"
    — Erica Miner, author of *Travels With My Lovers*

CREDENTIALS: Debbie Allen has authored four books including her award-winning book, *Confessions of Shameless Self-Promoters™*, that touts the science and strategies of effective self-promotion. Her ideas have been featured in magazines such as *Entrepreneur, Selling Power,* and *Sales & Marketing Excellence* as well as on dozens of syndicated TV and radio stations in the U.S. and Canada including Howard Stern.

AVAILABILITY: Arizona, nationwide by arrangement and via telephone
CONTACT: Debbie Allen, 1-800-359-4544; Debbie@DebbieAllen.com

Be Prepared When Reporters Call You Unexpectedly

Typically, radio producers and hosts reading *RTIR* will call you to make a telephone interview appointment. If you use your home telephone number in your contact information for *RTIR*, be aware that a producer might call you at home *live* on the air.

Also, if you list your home number as contact information in *Chase's Calendar of Events* in the course of creating a holiday, producers or hosts *will* more often than not call you live as they assume you are expecting media calls on the holiday you created.

When you get an unexpected live call, remember these two rules:

1. Write down the host and call letters of the station for your media kit.

2. Be certain to say your toll-free number or Website on the air. Motivate listeners to go there by suggesting a free download of valuable information.

Once You Book a Phone Interview With a Radio Producer

1. Verify the time, the time zone, and ask in advance if they can record and e-mail an audio copy of the interview. You may also wish to investigate ways of recording interviews via your phone and recording software or a simple recording device.

2. Verify how long you will be on the air.

3. Ask if it is okay to give out your toll-free number or Website at the end of the interview.

4. Ask if there will be commercial breaks.

5. Ask if it is okay to give a book or other product or service away.

Radio producers do not like a "pluggy guest" who acts as if she's giving a commercial instead of solid information. Yet, most hosts will allow you to give out your phone number and Website at the end of the show.

Preparing for Your Radio Interview

Once you have defined the interview date and time, invest in a telephone headset so your hands can be free to jot down notes as you speak.

Have your message points, supporting facts, and the sheet of questions you sent to the producer in front of you, along with a copy of your book with coded flags or paper clips marking key sections.

Also, keep the following points in mind:

> ❯ Plan to use a landline instead of a cell phone, and make sure the call-waiting feature is turned off.

> ❯ Have water in case your throat gets dry.

> ❯ If you have pets or children, make sure they do not enter the room while you are on the air and that they cannot be heard.

> ❯ In advance of the show, give a few friends or relatives the number of the show's call-in line and ask them to listen to the show and call to ask you a question when the host opens the line up for calls. Many listeners are reluctant to be the first one, and it can be embarrassing to wait for calls that never come.

❯ In advance of the show, personalize your interview by going on the Internet and finding the weather and local news in that city. Mentally assume you are in the studio with the host.

❯ Plan to call the host by his or her first name.

❯ When call-in guests ask questions, plan to write down and repeat their names as you answer.

How to Sell More Products and Services on the Radio

The best way to sell more products and services on the radio is to give great content and useful information in an upbeat, enthusiastic way. Following are a couple of techniques you can use to boost your sales, as well as get contact information from your listeners so you can contact them later:

1. **Offer a free item to all listeners.**

   It is important to offer something free to all listeners. The item can be as inexpensive as a tip sheet or as tangible as a free audiocassette. Typically, you would ask listeners to send you a self-addressed stamped envelope, stuff the freebie inside, then send it back to the listener.

2. **Create an on-air contest or quiz for a more expensive item.**

   The idea here is to generate excitement. Have you seen members of a studio audience go wild on TV shows like *The Price Is Right* when they win something?

   Use the excitement a contest creates to add momentum to your radio segment. Think of an item to give away that has value in the minds of your listeners, such as a book.

Rehearse How You Will End Your Radio Segment

If you are selling products, you want listeners to remember your e-mail address, Website, or toll-free number.

Remarkably, many people work very hard to get booked on the radio, but quickly (and often, inaudibly) race through their contact information so few can understand it, let alone remember it.

Here are two success tips to help your audience remember your information:

1. **Write out your contact information script and rehearse it long before the show.**

   Write down exactly what you will say, word for word, before your segment ends. Most producers will let you say your Website or toll-free number at the end of the show. They will say something like, "So where can our listeners find you?"

   This is your cue to say:

   "You can buy my book at *www.books.com*. That's *book* as in *look* with a dot-com extension.

   "You can also buy my books with a toll-free number. The number is (*say it slowly!*) 1-555-Luv-Books. Again, that is 1. 5. 5. 5. *L* as in love. *U* as in unicorn. *V* as in Valentine. Books."

2. **Have the host help you "ready the listener" for your contact information.**

   Before the show, ask the host if he or she could tell the audience to get out their pens and paper before the last commercial break, because you have some important information for them they will want to write down.

Scoring Brownie Points

Dave Shields, author of *The Race: A Novel of Grit, Tactics, and the Tour de France*, was able to create buzz and reach his target market of bicycling enthusiasts with savvy radio promotion. He's found that hosts keep him on the air twice as long when he makes the host look good. He does so by ending the interview with a sentence like, "I've set up a link where fans of (name the radio host you are speaking to) can purchase a book. I will donate a third of the price to (a charity related to some aspect of the book) and enter them to win a trip to (a winning prize related to some aspect of the book)."

After the break, give them the information you promised. Now they will have their pens and paper to write down your contact information.

Chapter Summary _____

1. Be proactive in seeking radio assignments.

2. Practice by calling into live call-in shows and voicing your opinion.

3. Listen to radio shows and analyze the best guests—and the worst ones.

4. Use a combination of phoning and e-mailing information to interest radio producers in your pitch.

5. Consider a service such as *Radio-TV Interview Report* to have producers call you.

6. Practice your key points before your interview.

7. Be certain you practice your close so your listeners can remember your contact information.

Chapter Assignments

❑ Make a firm date to call into one live call-in show this week. Listen to the show for a good half-hour before you call and write out the message you want to relay beforehand. Break your message down into three key points, and support each point with facts, statistics, and anecdotes.

❑ Record your interview if you can or have a friend listen and give you feedback. Was your voice confident? Was your message clear? Keep calling in to different shows until you can give a clear message on the air with confidence.

❑ Use the example of William Gordon's e-mail radio pitch as the basis for your own. Pique the producer's interest, then give your talking points.

❑ Consider what you can give away to create excitement on the air. If you are an author, give away a book. If not, perhaps there is a certificate you can give away for a service. Be creative.

❑ Send the producer a thank-you note and pitch yourself as a guest who is always available to be interviewed in the event of an emergency.

4

How to Create Celebrity Status via Television Interviews

When you can do the common things of life in an uncommon way, you will command the attention of the world.
—Thomas Carlysle, Author
(1795–1881)

In today's increasingly competitive world, television is the most powerful weapon in your arsenal for establishing yourself as the expert of choice. When clients and colleagues see *your face* in the same "magic box" usually occupied by movie stars and politicians, psychologically *you* take on the same celebrity cache.

Marilee Driscoll would have been yet another long term plan specialist if she had not decided to court the media, ultimately snaring a national interview on *The Early Show*, which gave her a national platform.

Mary Lou Andre's appearance on CNN further established her as a national wardrobe consultant and gave her enhanced credibility in her regional market of New England.

On a local level, Vicki Donlan's weekly appearances on New England Cable News gave her enhanced visibility as the (unseen) publisher of the monthly publication, *Women's Business*.

How to Make Your Media Appearances Work for You 24/7

Some people wonder if appearing on television is really worth the time, effort, and expense it might take to get booked. *"I'm only going to get three to six minutes,"* they grumble. *"Why bother? What if my target market isn't watching?"*

The value of a television appearance isn't the few minutes you spend chatting with the host. It is making your appearances work for you every hour of the day, 365 days a year through your collateral materials.

Driscoll, for example, knew that even if her target market missed her *Early Show* appearance, they could see the segment over and over via the video clip on her Website or read of her appearance in her collateral materials.

Management consultant Rebecca Morgan accepted an invitation to appear on *The Oprah Winfrey Show* even though she knew that by doing so she would not be putting herself in front of her target market of business professionals. Yet Morgan also knew that as everyone dreams of being an *Oprah* guest, appearing on the show will enhance her own prestige and she could parlay this coveted national appearance into more appropriate national shows.

Finally, she could make her *Oprah* appearance work for her 24 hours a day by listing this prestigious media appearance on her Website, and use the words "as seen on *Oprah*" on her business cards.

As seen on Oprah!

Morgan Seminar Group

1440 Newport Avenue
San José, CA 95125-3329
408/998-7977
Fax: 408/998-1742
800/247-9662
Rebecca@RebeccaMorgan.com
www.RebeccaMorgan.com

Rebecca L. Morgan, CSP, CMC
Speaker ▲ Seminarist ▲ Author

PRESENTATIONS:

Calming Upset Customers

Interpersonal Communication Savvy

TurboTime: Maximizing Your
Results Through Technology

The Power of Our Words

Time Management Triumphs

Professional Selling

BOOKS: (call us to order)

*Life's Lessons: Insights and
Information for a Richer Life*

*TurboTime: Maximizing Your
Results Through Technology*

Calming Upset Customers

*Professional Selling: Practical
Secrets for Successful Sales*

Inspiring Others to Win

*Speaking Successfully: 1001 Tips for
Thriving in the Speaking Business*

When national wardrobe consultant Mary Lou Andre was interviewed by CNN's Elsa Klensch, she was able to turn the pre-taped interview into a publicity bonanza by sending postcards of her forthcoming interview to her large mailing list of prospects, clients, colleagues, and media contacts. Even if few people on the mailing list actually tuned in to watch her on the show, by sending the postcard, Andre had cemented her status as a respected national expert and elevated her image.

Dressing Well ©

A Quarterly Publication of
Organization By Design

Special Announcement
Summer 1995

Organization By Design • 206 Marked Tree Road • Needham, Massachusetts   02192   *Telephone: 617-444-0140 • Fax: 617-449-9463*

*Mary Lou Andre
President and Founder*

This Just In . . .

On August 19th Mary Lou Andre will be featured on CNN's new series "All About Women" during the Cable News Network's 12:00 noon, 5:00 p.m. and 12:00 midnight newscasts. The piece will also air on Sunday, August 20th at 9:00 a.m.

Also watch for Mary Lou's fashion minutes airing each week on WHSH-TV, Channel 66, an affiliate of the Home Shopping Network.

Fall is just around the corner. Give us a call if you would like help organizing and shopping for your cool weather wardrobe. We welcome the opportunity to make you look and feel terrific!

Organization By Design is a wardrobe management company that helps women gain control over their wardrobes through closet organization, fashion consulting and personal shopping.

In addition to our private client services, we consult with corporations, providing them with professional dress seminars, casual day policy development & training and public appearance preparation. We also speak publicly to a variety of organizations.

Dressing Well is written and published quarterly by Mary Lou Andre to correspond with spring, summer, fall, winter and holiday wardrobing needs.

Please share your editions of *Dressing Well* with your friends and colleagues. For subscription information, call 617-444-0140 or 800-578-3770. You may also send the request in writing to OBD, 206 Marked Tree Road, Needham, Massachusetts 02192.

Television can turn you into a national expert. Even a single local appearance has the power to spawn national television interviews, print and radio interviews, speaking engagements, and even book deals.

Marisa, you may be thinking to yourself, *I see the value of TV. But I'm just an average person in business. You're saying I can get on national TV?*

Eileen Roth was also just an "average person in business" when she sought media attention to publicize her professional organizer business.

Without a publicist or any media experience, Roth was able to *book herself* on the *Today* show and *The Oprah Winfrey Show* with little more than free reference books at her local Chicago public library and a couple of stamps.

So can you!

In this chapter, we are going to explore the myriad of ways you can get booked on television shows in order to enhance your credibility, reach your target market, and position yourself as the expert of choice. You will learn easy, step-by-step techniques for generating your own pitch letters, using the same techniques as high-priced publicists. Finally, you will discover alternatives to professional PR services, including *pay for placement*, in which you pay a fee only when you are actually booked on a show.

Simple Secrets of Getting Booked on TV

As you must realize by now, the secret of getting booked on television is to make a connection between what you want to promote, events in the news, and a topic that would be of beguiling interest to the show's demographics.

Let's look at Eileen Roth's technique.

As a professional organizer new in the business, Roth was aware she'd need the media's help to build her business. A savvy client in the advertising business told Roth that she would need a "news hook" in order to attract the interest of a talk show producer.

Finding the News Hook

Why a news hook?

Simply telling a talk show producer you would like to be interviewed because you are a professional organizer, or a doctor, lawyer, or Indian chief for that matter, will generate a yawn.

Television is a highly visual medium, and producers want to book guests who will keep their viewers stimulated and engaged. Moreover, even though it is the producer's job to "produce" and put together segments of the show, you must be the one to sell him on what an asset you will be to the show. This doesn't mean just *selling yourself*; it virtually means putting the show together for the producer and helping him see how your segment can increase ratings.

As you brainstorm the form your pitch will take, realize that, above all, you must provide information that is of keen interest to the viewing audience. Moreover, your information should:

> Entertain the audience.

> Edify the audience (provide value so the audience will feel enriched and more knowledgeable by virtue of watching the segment).

> Increase the audience's awareness of new trends.

> Highlight new trends, holidays, or a seasonal focus.

Eileen Roth knew January was the premier month for carrying out New Year's resolutions. She learned about the wacky holidays featured in *Chase's Calendar of Events* and wanted to find an established holiday in January to use as a news peg to promote her service.

When she flipped through *Chase's Calendar of Events* at her local library and saw that National Clean Off Your Desk Day was celebrated in January, she decided to use this as her news hook.

As a first step, Roth wrote a news release and then sketched out some tips people could use to be more organized. Before sending the tips to the media, she tested them out with her local Toastmasters group.

"Forget tips; create *principles*," her Toastmasters buddies urged. Taking their advice to heart, Roth created a press release with six principles for organizing one's desk. Using a directory from the Chicago PR Society and the media directories located in her public library, she mailed off the principles and a personalized mail merge letter to 150 radio and TV stations.

Ten days later, Roth received a call inviting her to fly to New York and appear on the *Today* show with Bryant Gumbel to discuss National Clean Off Your Desk Day.

"I learned the importance of props that first appearance," Roth recalls, explaining that the producer sent her out to buy props that would be placed on a desk so she could verbally and visually walk the audience through the six principles of how to keep a clean desk. The appearance was so popular she was invited back six months later.

Shortly after her first *Today* show appearance, Roth was invited to appear on *The Oprah Winfrey Show*. For her *Oprah* appearance, Roth was sent to the home of a "pack rat" and given the challenge of organizing the woman's messy residence during the 60-minute span of the show while a second unit camera crew chronicled the tension-filled, ticking-clock action. Meanwhile, live on the *Oprah* set, Oprah and radio personality Dr. Laura Schlessinger discussed the mentality of a pack rat.

The confluence of publicity paved the way for the publisher John Wiley & Sons commissioning her to write *Organizing for Dummies*.

What's truly unique about this story is that Roth received *three national television* appearances, a book deal, and jump-started her business for little more than the cost of postage.

Developing an Action Plan

Now that you know the principles of getting booked on television, think about the best shows that would support your objectives. In addition to network shows, there are an increasing number of cable shows that may reach your target audience.

Find all viable shows by searching through media directories at the local library, or investing in resources such as *Bradley's Guide to the Top National TV Talk & Interview Shows* (*www.freepublicity.com/getontoptv*), which is a directory of shows with commentary and tips from producers on the best way to pitch.

Create a list of shows for which you would be an appropriate guest. Be sure to note the appropriate producer to pitch, as well as if the producer prefers the pitch via e-mail, snail mail, or fax. For example, even though *Good Morning America* is based in New York, the show asks that all pitches go to Bill Cunningham in their West Coast office via e-mail. Cunningham then forwards appropriate pitches to the appropriate New York segment producers, who will be in contact with you if the idea is of interest.

Some network morning shows have 17 producers, each responsible for a different type of segment, such as non-fiction books, fiction books, cooking, and so forth. If the directory does not make it clear, call the receptionist. Pitch the wrong producer or send your material in the wrong format, and your pitch will likely be deleted.

Studying the Shows

Now that you've looked through the directories and have targeted some viable shows, watch these shows with a pen and your notebook in hand. Look for the following:

❭ Do they feature guests similar to you? If so, note ways you are better and different from your competitors, as well as the name of the guest and date of the show (you will need this information for your pitch).

❭ Do the segments use visuals? If so, how often? How can you match or surpass the kinds of visuals used on the show.

❭ If you are an author, pay close attention to shows that feature authors. Note what makes the best author interviews interesting. Try to model their success. At the same time, keep a sharp eye out for author blunders and write down points to avoid.

❭ Observe if certain hosts commonly interview certain types of guests. If you fit into one specific category, mention that host's name in your pitch.

Creating the Pitch

Your pitch must be relevant to the audience and timely in that it reflects what's going on in the world today. Particularly in television, your pitch must have a strong emotional pull.

Make your pitch compelling and as emotional as you can given the subject matter. Though the ideal pitch is three short paragraphs (with Internet links as needed), you may want to go a bit longer in the case of an e-mail pitch to television producers by adding talking points or intriguing questions the host may wish to ask you.

Developing Talking Points for Your Pitch

One of the most important elements of your pitch letter or e-mail is listing enticing "talking points" that will motivate a producer to book you. The best way to begin the process of creating talking points is to watch the top-rated morning shows and see how other authors and experts get their points across.

An author might take the next step by going through his book and making note of every key concept. An expert might sit down with the major newspapers and create a bulleted list of how his business connects with what's being talked about in the news.

The next step is to shape these points in a way that would be enticing to a variety of producers. Employ the headline tactics you read about in Chapter 1, such as beginning with "5 Tips to _____," asking a question, or crafting a "how-to" headline that would solve a problem for the publication's target audience.

Your list of "generic" yet enticing talking points should be loaded onto your Website and serve as a link for producers who request an e-mail query.

If you have the luxury of sending the producer a print letter, take this concept a step further and tweak the talking points until they are a perfect match for the demographics of the show you are targeting.

Your Media Kit

Even if producers glance at your physical or online kit for five seconds, for better or worse, they judge your merit as a guest on the way it looks. Sloppy, unprofessional kits equal unprofessional guests. Attractively presented kits suggest attractive, well-put-together guests.

Be certain to make your media kit as professional looking as possible, which for physical media kits includes neat color clips and articles, and for online kits includes an attractive-looking page without broken links.

The only real advantage to a physical media kit is that when you know you will be sending it to a specific show, you can add extra material that underscores the reason why your segment needs to be broadcast for the show's target audience as soon as possible.

For example, let's assume you are a financial expert (with or without a book) who wants to educate viewers of a show with a large female audience that *if* they are going to get divorced, it's best to wait after they've been married for 10 years. The reason? Social security benefits kick in at the 10-year mark.

Supporting evidence can include a recent newspaper article focusing on the folly of a woman who divorced at the nine-and-a-half-year mark or a list of your clients who made this mistake and will be willing to come on the show with you and talk about it on the air.

To bolster your case, in advance of sending the material to the show, you might seek to publish in a newspaper a tip list with the headline, "Ten Things Women Must Know Before They Divorce," and include this tip sheet in your folder.

(More information on constructing online media kits can be found in Chapter 10.)

Arranging Your Material

Assemble your press material neatly in your two-pocket folder. If you are using folders from an office supply store, try to buy brightly colored folders with a glossy, coated finish. Personalize your folder by pasting a sticky-back photo of your book, photograph, or your company logo on the front cover.

Tami DePalma of the PR firm MarketAbility.com has a way of cutting various press materials in a layered fashion so that when a producer opens the folder, he can see all the materials at a glance.

Try to see if you can make this method work for you. Tuck your pitch letter (more on that in the following sections) in the right-hand pocket or, if there is nothing on the cover, paper clip your pitch letter to the front of your folder.

Your press release should be tucked into the left pocket, with your photograph in front of it. Most quality folders have an area on the right pocket designed to hold your business card. If your folder doesn't have this area, glue your card to the right pocket.

If you are including articles you've written or that have been written about you, consider having them printed in color for extra visual impact.

The Pitch Letter

Your pitch letter must be compelling enough to immediately grab the producer's attention. Furthermore, it should be written in a tone that matches the style of the show.

A good way to figure out how to formulate your pitch is to watch the show with specific attention to the "promos," or the promotions that remind the viewer to stay tuned because XYZ is coming up in the next segment. Train your ear to see how they position each segment to incite interest and inspire curiosity. Now, give your pitch the same flavor.

Your segment idea must figuratively pop off the written page. In words and phrasing, it should play out the way an actual segment would and excite the producer's imagination so she can "see" how the segment will look.

No matter the tone or subject matter of the show, your pitch must be dramatic and emotional. Adjust the level of drama up or down to suit the show you are pitching, but avoid writing anything that might put the producer to sleep. Your pitch, even to a number-crunching financial show, must stimulate the producer about the exciting possibilities your proposed segment offers. Let us assume that you were going to send a pitch to Bloomberg's *Sector Plays*. You look the show up in *Bacon's Media Directories* and find they are looking for industry experts to identify trends and investment opportunities and that they are trying to appeal to a national audience interested in daily financial news.

A great subject line would ask a question that draws a producer into the pitch, especially a question that evokes emotion through fear. The producer knows his audience watches the show because they are terrified of losing money in the financial markets. They invite experts on the show to speculate on trends before they happen so the audience can take quick action.

A subject line such as "Is the Telecommunications Industry Dead? 5 Warning Signs to Watch," followed by the warning signs in bulleted points and a paragraph describing the expert's platform and expertise, would be a riveting pitch because it allows the producer to see in his mind how the segment will play out.

Additional Materials to Include

Authors should include a copy of their book—possibly more copies if the title is so irresistible the office staff might take it home to read. Greg Godek, author of *1001 Ways to Be Romantic*, warns that secretaries and assistants often take his book home to show to their boyfriends and husbands and advises those with books that have similarly alluring titles to send many copies.

In addition to the book, send a videotape of yourself in an interview situation.

How to Create a Demo Video

National producers want to see videotape on prospective guests to ensure that they can handle themselves on the show.

What if you have not been on television before?

How do you submit a videotape that looks more professional than if your brother-in-law shot it?

You have two options. The first is to spend between $6,000 and $10,000 to have yourself professionally taped by a local video company. Be certain they have a professional-looking studio and demand references. In addition to hiring the crew and paying for editing, you will also have to pay for the services of a host to interview you.

The "free" option is to tap into your city's local access cable station and try to get one of the producers who hosts a talk-format show to interview you. You can find an access cable station by calling the Alliance for Community Media at 202-393-2650.

Virtually every city offering cable is mandated to also offer a community channel, where everyday people can create shows and interview guests.

While the facilities in these community stations vary in relation to the affluence of the community, almost all offer a professional "on-air" setup as you would see on a national TV news show, complete with an anchor desk, wireless microphones, a director, and more.

Brian Jud of Hartford, Connecticut, created his show, *The Book Authority*, on his local community channel and turned his series into a thriving business, including media training, products to help authors media train themselves, and a wide array of services to the self-publishing community. He welcomes authors passing through Hartford to contact him with regard to getting booked. In Los Angeles, Connie Martinson hosts a similar show titled *Connie Martinson Talks Books* and has interviewed a wide variety of celebrity authors, including Sidney Sheldon, Norman Mailer, and Mary Higgins Clark.

When you call a local access cable station, ask the receptionist which producers interview interesting guests and if you can snail mail a colorful flyer offering your services as a guest for them to post in the station.

Cable Access Interview Tips

Rehearse for your cable television interview using the points you will learn in Chapter 5. Be certain to bring a blank videotape to the show for duplication, as this will be the "tape" you will send producers.

Most stations also have the ability to record on mini DV tapes, which makes for easier editing if you have a home editing system or plan to have an editor edit your tape so it looks more professional.

Television Pitch Checklist

Before you send your pitch, verify the following:

1. **Spell the producer's name right.**

   "If I see my name misspelled, I toss the letter immediately," a producer states, admitting a pet peeve shared by many.

   It may seem a little thing, but producers are absolute sticklers for well-written pitch letters with their names spelled correctly.

2. **Verify the producer is still employed.**

   "Mail still comes to me addressed to my predecessor, and she left a year ago," complains an exasperated producer.

   In an industry where producers sort their mail over a trash can, producers are looking for the smallest excuse to trash your letter and reduce their workload.

3. **Verify you are pitching the appropriate producer.**

   It's always a good idea to verify that you are sending your letter to the correct segment producer.

4. **Establish relevance and timeliness.**

   Producers typically read e-mail releases with a forefinger on the delete key, skim faxes even as they are in the process of crunching them into a ball, and scan a mailed press release or letter over the circular file.

   What stops them from tossing the release forever?

   Two elements:

   1. The relevance of what you want to promote to their audience.
   2. The timeliness of your subject.

   Put yourself in the producer's position. Before sending your letter or release, give it a three-second scan the way a producer would, and ask yourself these questions:

   ❯ Is the release or information relevant to their publication or show?

   ❯ Does it offer information that their audience needs and values?

   ❯ Is the release or information timely?

   ❯ Does it tie in with what's in the headlines today?

   ❯ Does it tie in with the seasons or an upcoming holiday?

   If the material could have been used two weeks earlier or two weeks later, often it is tossed. You must work hard to make a strong case for why the producer and his audience needs the information now.

5. **Tweak your pitch, in both letter and e-mail forms, so it is personalized for the producer and show.**

When you write a personalized pitch letter, it tells the producer that you have done your homework and are familiar with the hosts, their personalities, their style, and the questions they typically ask.

6. **If appropriate, make specific mention of past shows.**

    If your pitch is similar to a previous guest, mention that guest and date of the show, but build a case for why you are better and different.

    You may say something to the effect of: "Like Guest X, I will speak on Y and Z, but my proposed segment also offers eye-catching visuals and an easy-to-remember acronym that helps the audience retain the information I will deliver."

7. **Brainstorm and spell out the "visual element" that could help turn channel surfers into viewers.**

    Television producers are visual thinkers. With the competition just a click away, producers know that they must give a basic interview a new form and dimension. This is why chefs *demonstrate* recipes instead of just talking about their book, and why interview-based shows like *The View* often feature makeovers and fashion shows.

8. **Condense your concept into an acronym.**

    An acronym is a word formed from the initials or other parts of several words. Depending on what you want to promote, you can use an acronym to your advantage. Using an acronym helps the audience remember your concept and, once again, helps a producer reading your pitch better visualize how your segment will play out on the air. It also elevates you above an expert who addresses similar issues without a memorable acronym.

9. **Consider making reference to how you will interact with a host.**

   If you are targeting a show and notice that a specific host works with a specific type of guest, help the producer visualize the segment. For example, a chef with a new cookbook might say, "Al Roker and I will make mouthwatering hot cross buns together."

Creating Follow-Up Phone Call Scripts for TV Producers

Calling simply to ask if they received your materials is ineffective. It's your responsibility to reawaken desire for your information.

On the day you will make follow-up calls, look again to your city or national newspaper to find "new news" you can link with your pitch.

Work out a script that works for personal contact as well as voice mail.

Try to get the producer live. If you can't leave a voice mail that sounds something like this:

"Hello. I am John Smith, 212-555-1212, calling to give you new information on the pitch I sent you on *Why Savvy Women Fail in Marriage*. Today, celebrity X just announced she was divorcing X, and this is a great news hook for the show. If you need more information, call me at 212-555-1212. I'll try you back next week."

If you don't hear from the producer after a second call, move on to another show.

Mailing Tips

If producers want to see your pitch and a media kit, looks count. Bob Frare, author of *Partner Selling*, has all his collateral materials match the cover of his book, including his media kit binders, his video and audio labels, his stationery, business cards, and even mailing labels.

Because you can't be there in person, you want to "look good in the mail" and connote a professional appearance.

Mailing your materials via FedEx is usually a good idea. When you are certain that your package had arrived on a certain date, wait three days before making the follow-up call.

Pay for Play

Professionals know that television interviews, especially on top shows, can catapult their business to the major league. Yet not everyone has the time or resources to create the perfect pitch and place "dial and smile" follow-up calls, especially if their main focus is on servicing existing clients.

Traditional PR agencies can actively work to get you media placements but, according to the rules of the Public Relations Society of America (PRSA), are not at liberty to promise you anything. So this could leave you paying a six-month minimum retainer plus related fees with no placement to show for it.

Annie Jennings of one of the leading national PR firms, Annie Jennings PR, offers a high-performance "pay for placement" publicity program in which she invests in her clients first by creating a variety of publicity materials, including her famous "segment style press release," and pitches to the client's dream list of shows and publications. If none of the shows or media outlets bite, the client pays no fee.

When the client gets a booking, she pays Annie Jennings PR a placement fee dependent on several factors, including the magnitude and content of the media placement, space, circulation, and more. Annie Jennings PR guarantees the media placement to air or print so, if a client is bumped, canceled, or edited out, she is not responsible for paying a fee. The firm absorbs the media risk and bankrolls its clients for print and TV.

Chapter Summary

1. The value of your television appearance is more than the three to six minutes you are on the air, as you can list your appearance in your online press room and also show a video clip, audio clip, and print clip on your Website.

2. You can promote an upcoming TV segment with a postcard targeted to your prospects, clients, colleagues, and other media.

3. Hook your news onto a news peg, but ensure that it is of broad and immediate interest to your target audience.

4. Study the news shows and make sure your pitch is appropriate.

5. Realize the importance of emotion in creating your pitch.

6. Personalize your pitch for each individual show.

Chapter Assignments

❏ This week, identify three television talk shows on which you can appear.

❏ Watch the shows and identify the most strategic way to make a pitch.

❏ Begin to assemble your media kit.

5

How to Media Train Yourself

> *The one function that
> TV news performs very
> well is that when there is
> no news, we give it to
> you with the same
> emphasis as if it were.*
>
> —David Brinkley,
> Acclaimed Broadcast
> Journalist
> (1920–2003)

Nicholas Boothman, author of *How to Connect in Business in 90 Seconds or Less*, recalls that when he first began promoting his book, a reporter from the Canadian nightly news thrust a giant microphone in his face and asked, "What's your book about?"

"How long do you have?" Boothman shot back.

It was then that Boothman realized he needed media training.

"You have to answer that kind of question in a sound bite," he later realized.

Why Media Train?

Some media historians date the need for media training back to the televised Nixon-Kennedy political debate of 1960. For the first time, the bulk of mainstream America could view presidential candidates giving their message points in real time, instead of reading about their platform in the newspaper.

While the candidates' message points remained as they had been in print, new wild cards included body language as each reacted to points made by their opponent and the sincerity projected through eye contact as they looked America straight into the camera lens and made their solemn promises.

When you are on television or speaking on the radio, your "essence"—the sum of who you are, what you stand for, and all that you've worked toward—are up for immediate scrutiny, instant replay, and chatter by colleagues, clients, and competitors.

All is fair in love and publicity, but many celebrities are haunted by past interviews repeated endlessly on stations such as *E! Entertainment Television*, while non-celebrities with good information to share but without adequate media training have been devastated to see that their broadcast interview did not capture them in the best light.

Media training can help you:

> Keep the interview under *your* control.

> Effectively package and present your message.

> Project authority and credibility.

> Show clients and prospects how professionally you handle the media.

> Position yourself as a powerful media liaison.

> Match wits with shrewd reporters and bulldog news hosts.

❯ Deliver the sound bites the media demands.

❯ Learn how to convey a clear, concise message.

❯ Ensure your message is understood as you intended.

❯ Develop confidence during TV and radio broadcasts.

❯ Learn how to bridge difficult questions.

❯ Deflect hostile interviewers.

❯ Give the kind of performance that gets you invited back.

❯ Understand the mistakes that can get you blacklisted.

In this chapter, we will explore the elements necessary for an effective broadcast interview, as well as how to shape your message in an interview with print journalists. Media training is necessary, but expensive, so you will also learn the step-by-step process of media training *yourself*, as well as unconventional and low-cost ways to ensure you are "media ready."

Successful Interviews Are Message-Driven

What makes an interview successful? The answer is getting your message across and understood by the target audience.

To better prepare yourself, at the time you are booked, ask the following questions:

❯ What is the purpose of the interview?

❯ What is your role in the interview or on the panel?

❯ Will anyone else be interviewed?

> What is the format of the show?

> What is the length of the show?

Understanding the Interview Process

Every interview situation is comprised of the same elements. Producers of radio and TV talk shows want guests who can edify and entertain their audiences. Segment producers who book guests know that their jobs are on the line with every interview.

In broadcast media, line producers are constantly monitoring a live segment with an eye towards a device that tells them if their audience is increasing, staying put, or changing channels. When the producer sees people dropping out, he issues an order via the host's earphone to cut the segment short.

Producers want you to be fabulous. Realize, too, that being "fabulous" might mean something different on *Good Morning America* than it would on *Scarborough Country*. One show might want guests who are upbeat, positive, and "nice," while other shows might want a gutsy, controversial guest who isn't afraid to be outrageous and speak his mind.

Be aware that some media people have their own agendas. They invite you on a show with a hidden plan to get you to say or admit to something, either to sensationalize an issue or motivate viewers to cast a suspicious eye towards your industry or your own business.

Print journalists sometimes might pretend to be your friend or soften you up to admit things you wouldn't. At times, you might feel like saying something "off the record." Resist the temptation. Nothing is ever off the record as far as the media is concerned, and your words can come back to haunt you.

Can an Expert Wing an Interview?

A hallmark of entrepreneurs and successful businesspeople is their ability to charm and endear themselves to people around them. In life, they have learned to improvise and have found it's worked well for them.

Yet, it is not a good idea to "wing" a media interview. Potential consequences of having no planned message are:

> ❯ You will look scattered and ill-prepared.

> ❯ You will be robbed of your credibility.

> ❯ The interviewer will be able to use you for his own purposes and agenda.

> ❯ You will be left without facts, statistics, stories, and data you will need to present a convincing argument for your case.

> ❯ You will be robbed of a strong call to action.

Packaging and Selling Your Message

Define your message:

1. What key information do you want to relay?

2. Who is the audience who will hear your message? What are their common interests?

3. What action do you want them to take as a result of hearing your message?

4. Given the specific interests of this targeted audience, what facts, statistics, or anecdotes will best help them see the importance of your message and take the next step?

It's good to note that messages do not necessarily have to be delivered in a specific order. If the host begins with a question that is best addressed by your third message point, go ahead and start there.

Tips for Message Point Creation

Ask yourself:

1. What do people need to believe and care about in order to become absorbed in the issue I am discussing?

2. What obstacles do I need to overcome to get people engaged?

3. How can I support my message with facts, statistics, and anecdotes?

4. What do I want people to do as a result of my message?

Practice Message Discipline

Message discipline is when you know your message so well that you can deliver three key message points to a new acquaintance as you ride the elevator. The same discipline holds true when you stay on message during a talk show.

How to Media Train Yourself

The best advice is offered by Connie Dieken, an award-winning news anchor turned media trainer. "Be a color commentator," she says, using a sports metaphor, "not a play-by-play announcer."

This means:

> ❯ Your answers to questions should be colorful sound bites of 20 words or less.

> ❯ Do not ramble—stay focused and on message.

In this section, we will talk primarily about television, but much of it can be applied to radio as well.

Your first step should be to make a practice out of watching guests on top talk shows. Buy an inexpensive notebook for this purpose and begin to keep a journal of what TV guests do right—and mistakes they make you can learn from.

Begin with their core message point. How did they support their message? Did they keep on message or did they allow the host to take them away from their key point? If they kept on message, what techniques did they use to change the subject back to their agenda?

Notice if the guests made gestures. If so, were they distracting, or did the gestures help underscore their message? From the guest's body language, did you sense that they were comfortable and at ease, or nervous?

In a two-dimensional medium like television, the viewing audience pays close attention to words, but even more attention to body language. If the guest says he's delighted to be on the show but is stiff and tense, the message is, "I'm very tense about being on the show."

Body Language

Body language is a crucial element in good communication one rarely considers when practicing for a TV interview. To better see and study the body language of television guests, turn off the sound as you view the visual. Look at the gestures of a guest. Is he crossing his arms in front of his chest? Does he seem nervous? Is his posture upright and smile genuine?

You will probably agree that body language speaks louder than words. Try to create your own dictionary of body language. When the sound is turned off, what actions characterize a "confident guest"? Is it a guest that smiles often and shakes the host's hand vigorously? Without hearing the conversation, what shows you he is *confident*? What about a nervous guest? Note the characteristics.

At the same time, with the sound turned off, what makes you decide if you *like* a guest or not? Can you also get a sense of if the host likes the guest or merely tolerates him?

Eye contact with the host, smiling, and nodding are all good. Whether the guest looks at the audience to make eye contact and smiles depends on the show and the tone of the guest's information. On a talk show like *The Ellen DeGeneres Show*, in which Ellen interacts with the studio and home audience a great deal, the guest may be able to get away with smiling and looking at the audience if he is in the midst of a funny story. Producers will tell you what is appropriate and where to look as they brief you and conduct a pre-interview before the show.

One of the most effective and least utilized tools to employ on interviews is mastering the power of the pause. This is particularly useful when the interviewer throws a difficult or hostile question at you and you need time to think.

Many guests, their nerves already tightly stretched, gush out an inappropriate answer to a difficult or challenging question because they don't take that quick few seconds to think and rephrase their question (see page 106).

Scandal, Disaster, Intrigue

Have you noticed that the news media love to cover disasters? Whenever there is a fire or flood, the news is there to cover it. And if it's a case of a car chase involving the police, many stations have an alert system for viewers.

Scandals and disasters are media favorites because they grab a viewer's emotions. The same principle on a lower scale is why hosts sometimes shake things up with a challenging question.

Controversy sells.

Researchers have discovered that when a viewer is channel surfing, they will usually pause to watch a show with people engaged in a strong emotion, especially if that emotion is conflict and opposition.

This is one of the reasons why, if you are pitching a panel to a top television show, it's always good to include an expert whose belief is contradictory to your own.

Speak, Spin, or Stonewall: Handling Hostile Interviewers

Knowing that controversy sells, hosts like to sneak a difficult question in for the same reason. It has nothing to do with their feelings for you or what you represent; it's just a tactic to provide a balanced view and stir emotions in the process. Also, some hosts are known for their antagonistic approach to guests, so if you book yourself on one of these shows, be especially vigilant about being well prepared.

When handling hostile interviews:

> ❭ Don't feel you have to answer the question as posed.

> ❭ Use bridge tactics.

> Think of the worst question you could be asked and rehearse your answers in advance.

> Reframe negative questions.

> Have data handy to reinforce credibility.

Imagine the Worst Question an Interviewer Can Ask

One of the best ways to prepare is modeled on a tactic used by the U.S. White House before a press event. In one long-ago administration, the chief of staff would ask all White House employees to submit the three most challenging or hostile questions any reporter could ask the president. Then, he would read the questions to the president and they would work out natural-sounding answers that made him sound like a good guy.

Of course, these answers would be filled with facts, statistics, and evidence that was researched in advance.

Because you can never be 100 percent sure of any media person's agenda, it's best to predict the worst question they can ask you in advance and have facts and statistics available to support your claim.

Also, don't feel you have to answer the question exactly as posed. Instead, use it as an opportunity to address the general topic.

Rephrasing the Question Is One Way to Control the Interview

Feeling compelled to answer any question addressed to them, some guests automatically gush out an answer without pausing and thinking of a better way to come across as polite, yet stay on message.

One way of answering is to simply rephrase the question. Begin this tactic with, "I think what you're asking is...," and then give one of your message points, supported by the evidence you have collected to support it.

Other transition or bridge points can begin this way:

> ❯ "Good question! The most important thing to remember is...."

> ❯ "Great question! Sometimes people ask me...."

> ❯ "That's a good question! Before I answer, I'd like to go back to my earlier point...."

When you do make your point, be certain to underscore it with facts, statistics, and anecdotes.

Practice Via Role-Play With a List of Questions

Many radio show hosts, as well as TV hosts, memorize or read from the questions you supply them. If you have prepared such a list, ask a friend to role-play with you and ask you questions. If you have an audio- or video-recording device, so much the better. Give the exercise a more dynamic flair by asking your friend to take on the characteristics of several real-life television hosts, such as Jane Pauley or Matt Lauer. Ask your friend to surprise you by being aggressive, demanding, even hostile.

Focus on:

> ❯ Answering questions in 20 seconds or less.

> ❯ Getting your message points across.

> ❯ Adding supporting evidence of your claim.

> ❯ Producing quotable sound bites.

Creating and Delivering Juicy Sound Bites

What is a sound bite, you may wonder, and why do I even need to concern myself with one?

Connie Dieken, an award-winning TV news anchor, explains that when she was looking for a great sound bite for a segment she was producing, she would put the cameraman's live footage into the edit bay and turn off the sound. Let's assume the cameraman had collected footage of man-on-the-street commentary in the aftermath of a fire. Dieken would fast-forward until she found a strong emotion on a person's face. Then she knew that whatever that person had to say would be a great sound bite.

Today, Dieken media trains a wide variety of professionals through her *Communicate Like a Pro* programs. One of the things she does in the course of her program is to train people how to create colorful, memorable sound bites. Here are a few of her suggestions:

> ❯ Use visual, vivid words such as "snowballed" or "skyrocketed."

> ❯ Use words that are emotion-based or conjure up an emotion.

> ❯ Use or start sentences with action verbs.

> ❯ Build a metaphor. Make it understandable for everyone. Enable it to relate to their needs.

> ❯ Transmit a sound bite that is memorable.

In her media training, Dieken works with clients to find three keywords they want an audience to remember about their topic. Sometimes the sound bite can rhyme, but it must form a very vivid, specific mind picture.

Media Training for Radio

Debbie Allen, national speaker and author of *Confessions of Shameless Self Promoters*, recalls that when Howard Stern booked her for an interview, her immediate reaction was, "He's going to beat me up!"

She sought training help from a friend who'd been on the *Howard Stern Show* for 90 minutes. As a result of her *Stern* appearance, her book was the Amazon best-seller that day.

How to Get Help With Media Training on a Budget

Professional help is always valued and worth the price. However, few people can afford the high fees, which can amount to more than $5,000 a day.

Beyond training yourself, what are alternative options?

Victoria Moran, best-selling author of *Lit From Within* and several other books that have made her an *Oprah* favorite, suggests that you begin very simply by observing yourself in any store's security camera. If you have never been on camera, just wave hello to yourself.

Next, take advantage of acting classes and improv classes offered by adult education centers in your city. According to Moran, improv classes help you feel comfortable with being put on the spot and answering correctly.

One of the most positive things you can do for yourself is to try to get interviewed on your city's cable access channel. Producers are frequently looking for good guests.

Preparing for Your Interview

Even though the producer has your question sheet, be prepared in the event they ask their own questions. Read over your press material. Authors, it may have been a long time since you wrote your book, so read it again and arm yourself with anecdotes and other information from the book. Brainstorm all the questions the interviewer could possibly ask, and arm yourself with good answers and colorful sound bites.

For every one of your message points, try to think of at least two anecdotes to help the audience map your message to their own experience.

Be familiar with who your interviewer is. Watch or listen to their shows. Get a feeling for the kinds of questions they ask. Try to dig up some personal information about them that you can use in small talk, such as a hobby.

What to Wear on the Set

Dress how you want to be perceived and match your area of expertise. For example, chefs should wear a toque. Professionals should wear a suit if this fits their identity. The best suit has a strong shoulder line to add authority and should be accessorized with a high-contrast shirt or blouse. Beware of wearing jewelry that makes noise, as the microphone is very sensitive.

Women, if you have long hair, keep it up or away from your face. Consider professional styling for a smoother, neater look. Makeup is usually provided on the set.

If you wear glasses, invest in lenses that reduce glare.

What to Be Aware of During Your TV Interview

Many people feel a bit nervous on their first interview. It's natural, because it is an unfamiliar situation. Practicing in front of a small audience such as a cable access station can do wonders to prepare you for the big day.

Arrive early and act with confidence. Producers and others on the set may be observing you to see the kind of guest you will be.

Once on the air:

> 〉 Assume you are live on camera at all times. Keep your head up and posture straight. You may not realize when the camera begins to roll.

> 〉 Smile. If you don't, the two-dimensional nature of the television screen means you risk people thinking you are angry or depressed.

> 〉 Use your host's first name (if this is customary for the show) to create a bond.

> 〉 Do not move around. Keep gestures small.

> 〉 Sit on the hem of your jacket, if possible, to keep the line of the shoulder neat and straight.

> 〉 Do not touch your hair or face. Restrain yourself from making nervous gestures.

> 〉 Watch your posture. If your posture is sloppy, it telegraphs that you are sloppy about your message.

> 〉 Keep your tone friendly and conversational, speaking to the host and sharing a tip as if with an old friend.

> 〉 Keep your answers short and focused. Less than 20 seconds is maximum.

> 〉 Do not over-answer. Make your point and be silent.

> 〉 If the host asks a question you can't answer, try to bridge or transition to another topic. Don't

ever make anything up or speculate without the facts in front of you.

> Do not use jargon, acronyms, or words above the heads of your audience. You will come across as pompous.

> Avoid saying "no comment." Either bridge to a better topic or say it's personal.

> If asked several questions at once, choose the question you want to answer, and reply, "That's a lot of questions. But to answer your question on X...."

> If on a panel, don't wait to be invited to speak. Jump in and get your message across.

> Enumerate. As you make points, hold up a finger. When you give a short, punchy sequence of points, it makes it harder to be edited out of a taped segment.

After the interview, send a thank-you note to the producer and host, as well as any other person who paved the way for your success.

Chapter Summary

1. Media training helps you keep the interview under your control.

2. Media training helps you package and present your message.

3. All successful interviews are message-driven.

4. In television, your body language rings truer than your vocalized message.

5. Practice transitioning to deflect a hostile interviewer.

6. A smile goes a long way in endearing yourself to an audience.

Chapter Assignments

❏ This week, plan time to create your core message and break it down into three key message points.

❏ Think of ways to support each of the three message points through facts, statistics, and anecdotes.

❏ Keep a notebook so you continually add anecdotes and facts. *Always be on the lookout for fresh material.*

❏ Sound bites are golden, and as they are often the only element ever used in an interview, create and perfect them on a daily basis.

❏ Before your first interview, brainstorm the most challenging question an interviewer could possibly ask you and then decide how you would answer it.

6

Creative Networking and Marketing Techniques to Build Buzz

> *It's only shallow people who do not judge by appearances.*
>
> —Oscar Wilde, Dramatist, Novelist, and Poet (1854–1900)

How far would you go to make the right impression at a networking event?

Most people might agree they would smile more, show an interest in others, and avoid pigging out at the buffet.

Mary Lou Andre sold her wedding dress.

Today, Andre is a nationally recognized wardrobe consultant and author of the best-selling book *Ready to Wear: An Expert's Guide to Choosing and Using Your Wardrobe*, but years ago she was a young woman with an empty bank account and a strategic plan for launching her career.

"I had very little money when I was first starting out, but knew the importance of projecting a professional image. The sale of my wedding dress allowed me to spend $200 a week attending different networking events, where I would sit at a table, deliver my elevator speech, and collect business cards. Then I would go home and write personal notes to the people whose business cards I collected."

Andre's strategic use of networking to instantly launch her career paid off in the form of loyal clients, national recognition, major national television appearances, and well-paid corporate speaking engagements.

In this chapter, you will learn everything you need to know about successful networking, including how to convey a confident image, why appearances count, how to communicate through clothing and collateral materials, and the secret of turning paper business cards into flesh and blood allies.

Networking as a Way of Life

"Networking is really a way of life," says Vicki Donlan, founder and publisher of *Women's Business Boston*. "I grew up watching my father talk to everyone, even to other tables at a restaurant. You never know who will become your next alliance. Emulating my father's technique helps me find advertisers for the paper and allows it to prosper."

In her introduction to this book, Susan RoAne, author of the best-selling *How to Work a Room*, provides a great example of the power of networking when she recalls our "cute meet" in the ladies room of a Chicago hotel during a media conference. Little did either of us know that by walking me over to her table filled with friends from her National Speakers Association, I would join and gain visibility in this organization and ultimately change my career.

Marcia Yudkin, a New England-based marketing consultant and author of *6 Steps to Free Publicity*, carries her books with her everywhere. People who end up buying her books often end up hiring her as a consultant or for a speaking engagement, or refer her to other clients.

Debbie Allen, author of *Confessions of Shameless Self Promoters*, says that when she goes to networking events she asks the other person to tell her about their business. When she senses a connection, she says, "I'd like to help you be more successful. I see us doing referrals, exchanging leads back and forth, marketing to the same customer base," and so forth. By looking for an alliance right away, Allen is able to amass an army of foot soldiers who spread the good word about her business while she does the same thing for theirs.

Confronting Networking Resistance

Why does networking seem like such a chore?

"I feel like I'm being scrutinized and sized up," says Amy, a graphic designer.

In a way, she's right. Scientists have recently discovered that when we meet someone new, our minds take in more than 100 messages per second about that person on a subconscious level.

Like a high-speed computer, we subconsciously scan others for "clues" that signal if a given individual is trustworthy or if we should be on our guard—an atavistic throwback from our caveman days.

And don't forget the "new kid at school" scenario. Lois Lindauer, founder of LLL Searches, vividly remembers entering a networking event at the prestigious Boston Club, the area's largest organization for high-achieving executive and professional women: "Everyone was kissing and hugging each other hello. I felt like an outsider."

Happily, that horrible feeling motivated Lindauer to join the nominating committee and ultimately become president of the organization, giving her a premier position among professional women in Boston and paving a successful career path.

Getting a Return on Investment From Your Networking Ventures

Networking is expensive and time-consuming, with no guaranteed return on investment. How can you best strategize about the best ways to show some result from your effort?

Choose your events carefully. Mary Lou Andre attended events suggested by her informal board of advisers. She knew she struck gold when she attended a chapter meeting of New England Women Business Owners (NEWBO) and quickly saw that this group of female business owners was her target market.

"I took the member directory and put everyone on my print newsletter mailing list," Andre recalls, in order to create awareness for her company, Organization by Design.

Andre also made it a point to become active and visible in the organization.

"Just showing up for meetings is important. I volunteered my time, did PR and marketing for events, and donated gift certificates for two hours of my services. Winners of the certificates hired me on a permanent basis and furthered word of my business."

Venture Out of Your Niche

Sometimes it can be good to venture out of your niche. Nancy Michaels, marketing expert and author of *Perfecting Your Pitch*, tells the story of an interior designer who began to attend networking events for lawyers under the theory that lawyers made good money but were so overworked, they probably didn't have time to arrange their own living space and would need her services. She was right, and her efforts paid off.

How to Turn a Strategic Lunch or Dinner Into Opportunity

Nancy Michaels scored big-time when, during a networking and fundraiser event, she saw a sign-up sheet to bid on lunch with Office Depot CEO Bruce Nelson. Even though winning the bid would require a four-digit investment, Michaels thought it a terrific opportunity.

As a result of being the highest bidder on that lunch, she:

❯ Gave 75 in-store Office Depot seminars in six months.

❯ Pitched and won the opportunity to give Webcast seminars on the Office Depot Web Cafe.

Michaels also credits savvy networking with helping her secure a monthly column with *Entrepreneur* magazine. She had been sitting next to editor Rieva Lesonsky after a speaking engagement at Babson College in Boston. Michaels introduced herself and kept in touch with Lesonsky, sending her articles and resources, and once again found herself sitting next to her on a Back on Track America tour where they were speaking on the same panel. They had dinner, and in the end, her column for *Entrepreneur* was secured.

In a similar fashion, celebrity chef Todd English found himself sitting next to the Ocean Spray CEO during a fundraiser. When the CEO told English how much he enjoyed his Charlestown restaurant, Olives, English suggested that if he loved it so much, he should sponsor his television cooking show. That show paved the way for a variety of restaurant concepts and product lines, as well as enhanced fame.

The stories above prove to underscore the point that if you don't ask, you don't get.

Use Visualization to Boost Your Self-Confidence

Aside from appearance, people at networking events consciously or subconsciously tap into your level of self-confidence.

Before you can "be" you must be able to "see."

The most successful people on the face of the earth tap into this power to manifest and project success.

Conrad Hilton, great-grandfather to the celebrity *du jour* Nikki Hilton and the founder of Hilton Hotels Corporation, came across a picture of the Waldorf Hotel in 1931, two years after the Great Depression, when creditors were beating down his doors. Financing a new acquisition was impossible, yet Hilton was so determined to buy the Waldorf, he slipped the picture under the protective glass top of his desk where it would always be within his field of vision.

By 1949, the Waldorf was his.

Visualization is a powerful tool.

In fact, researchers have discovered that our dreams, our fantasies, our actual memories, and movies we have seen are all in the same area of the brain. This explains why we often can't remember if we experienced something in real life or saw it in a dream or movie.

Before networking events, use the power of visualization to "see" yourself as dynamic, self-confident, and successful, and you will be well on your way to achieving it in reality.

Pre-Event Brainstorming

Before you go to an event, you must strategize ways to get the most out of your investment of time and money. Go over your goals and write down what you hope to achieve. Is there a speaker whom you want to meet? Are you shy and wish there was someone to introduce you around?

If so, ask meeting officers or organizers to introduce you at networking events in advance.

Virtually every association has a board, and on that board sits someone with the title of "VP Member Relations." Their job is to make new members feel at home and turn visitors into members by introducing them to key people and other officers in the organization. At the very least, an association or organization should have a paid chapter administrator who is responsible for arriving early, making nametags, and checking guests off the list, among other duties.

Well in advance of the event, call the member relations officer or chapter administrator to explain you are new, will be attending alone, and will be so grateful if someone could tell you more about the organization and introduce you to a few people. If you are shy, this is a great way to kick the meeting off to an excellent start.

Strategize Ways to Meet VIPs

Debbie Allen, author of *Confessions of Shameless Self Promoters*, knew that Robert G. Allen (no relation) was coming to Dallas, her place of residence, to give a talk. Knowing that his name carried major weight in many industries, she arrived early, her arms exhausted by carrying the weight of his books.

As she predicted, she was the first attendee to arrive and introduced herself, explaining that she was his biggest fan and, by the way, would he autograph her collection of his books?

Robert G. Allen signed, and was so flattered he agreed to provide an endorsement for Debbie Allen's book, thus paving the way for more credibility and visibility for Debbie Allen.

Association events often feature monthly meetings with celebrity speakers. Celebrities (whether within our industry or on the silver or political screen) can enhance our credibility by endorsing products or simply by being seen talking with them.

If you attend an association event exclusively to press the flesh and get on the radar screen with a celebrity, begin planning as soon as the event is announced. You may be disappointed if you simply hoped you would bump into them at the event and they would have time to chat.

E-mail the speaker or celebrity in advance, explain you would like to get to know them, and ask if you can have five minutes of his time before the event.

According to Vicki Donlan of *Women's Business*, one of the mistakes neophytes typically make at networking events is to invite someone to breakfast, lunch, or dinner without explaining why or what kind of information they want to receive.

"People are very busy, so it's important to be clear, open, and up front about what you want from them," says Donlan, explaining that, while she is open to helping people with contacts or other information, often it is best done at her computer. "If someone needs help finding a job, I could be of more service if they sent me their resume than if I sat with them during an hour at breakfast."

Keep a Straight SPINE at a Networking Event

Yes, posture is important. But when I give talks on networking, I found SPINE a convenient acronym to encapsulate the key concepts and "do's and don'ts" of attending a networking event:

1. **S = *Strategy*.**

   Consider that a networking event is not the place to "sell," but rather a place to develop your platform and position yourself as an expert in your field. Your first step is to be clear about what you want to achieve at the event. Don't leave the house until you know why you are going and who or what kind of people you need to meet. Look ahead to the next three to six months and ask yourself what specific person or types of people you will need to meet in order to build your business.

   Small business expert Denise O'Berry mentions she had a client who loved her women's groups. "But by attending, she wasn't networking with influencers who could connect her with her target market," says O'Berry, who finally persuaded the woman to find networking opportunities more conducive to getting leads and clients.

2. **P = *Partnerships*.**

Consider seeking out people with whom you can see a mutually beneficial relationship. Strategize about the ways that you can work together to add value to a specific client or industry, or act as a source or referral to one another.

In his book, *The Anatomy of Buzz*, Emanuel Rosen describes a type of person called a "connector." This person knows everyone and is at the center of everything. You can usually recognize a connector because he is surrounded by people at networking events. Typically, they are on the board of the organization. Getting involved in the organization is one way to meet them. Another is to make yourself memorable by sending them an item of interest.

3. **I = *Image*.**

The eyes trump the ears. Before people can actually *hear* what you have to say, they use their eyes to verify that you are a credible person to be dealing with.

An accountant once went for a job interview. Though he was qualified, the head of the department did not hire him. Why? "His shoes were run down," said the boss. "If the guy can't pay attention to a simple detail like that, how can he focus on financial details?"

"You represent your personal brand," notes national wardrobe consultant Mary Lou Andre. "The first thing I tell my clients is that they should think about clothing as *communication vehicles* rather than fashion choices. Many people spend massive amounts of time, energy, and money selecting the right logo, business cards, and stationery, but forget that in face-to-face encounters, your clothing is a projection of your personal brand."

Andre practices what she preaches. Part of the proceeds from the sale of her wedding dress went to invest in two "perfect" networking suits so that she could project the professional image she would manifest for her clients.

"People judge by appearance," says Denise O'Berry, president of the Small Business Edge Corporation. "People have an expectation of how someone who is successful in a given area would dress."

"Sometimes," adds Chris Vasiliadis, owner of self-promotion firm Signature Faces, "you see a hairdresser at networking events, her hair a mess. It makes a person wonder how she can expect to attract clients if she can't do her own hair."

Diane Danielson, founder of the Downtown Women's Club, always looks exceptionally well put together. Dressing for the day is a symbolic activity, because she feels herself to be a role model for young women trying to make it in today's corporate world.

4. **N = *Nerve*.**

Be bold! Seize the moment. If given a choice, it's best to plan your introduction by doing background research into the person or issue. But there are those "hit-or-miss" times in life when you have only one choice: either act immediately or lose the opportunity forever.

5. **E = *Exit*.**

In polite society, it is considered improper—even rude—to exit a conversation after only six minutes. But at the six-minute mark at a networking event, it's time to exchange cards and move on.

If you feel qualms about this, realize that you are doing your partner a favor by helping them meet more contacts. Simply say, "It was nice to meet you" and then exchange cards, or suggest you walk over to the buffet table together (where you will quickly meet other people).

Listening Skills

One way to encourage a person to talk is via an open-ended question. Resist the temptation to ask questions that could be considered personal or so rapid-fire they seem more like a form of interrogation.

Also, don't allow your eyes to wander the room as you listen. Hungry and bored, some people make the mistake of looking over their shoulder at a waiter bearing food or for someone more important as they pretend to listen. Train yourself to focus exclusively on the person you are speaking with.

Apocryphal or not, it's always good to listen more than you speak. The other person will like you for it, and you will learn more about the other person.

Business Card Etiquette

Consider a business card an extension of yourself. Jane Wilson, founder of Boston Women Communicators, whose organization sponsors networking events every month, has much to say about the proper way to exchange them:

"Do not grab someone's card as if it is not an item of interest. Look at the design. Notice the person's title. Look at the card as a tool to help remember their name. Make a mental note of an unusual spelling."

Wilson has seen many networkers take a card, curl it up as they speak, or shove it into a suit pocket without looking at it.

When it comes to entering the cards into her database, Wilson prefers to do this manually rather than using a device such as CardScan. This way, she can once again associate the name with the card.

Vicki Donlan, publisher of *Women's Business*, has an innovative way of handling cards. In addition to her contact management system, she has several old-fashioned Rolodexes in her office where she stores the cards. A few times a year, she spins through her Rolodexes and keeps in touch with her contacts. When a relationship is built with a contact in her Rolodex, at this point she transfers the contact to her contact management system.

Creating Vibrant Self-Introductions

You eyeball a key person you need to meet at a networking event. You say your name, reach to shake his hand—then what? How do you introduce your business?

The best self-introductions are heard as *juicy bites of sound*. You shake hands and give a short, snappy, 10-word sentence of what you do.

Deliver a boring (or worse, *rambling*) description of what you do for a living, and people will mentally zone out.

Take a tip from radio scriptwriters who have this test for their material: Make sure your radio spot is important, scary, funny, or interesting within the *first five seconds*. Why? Otherwise, folks would change channels or zone out.

Make It Easy on Others to Remember Your Name

When you introduce yourself to someone, enter a small group, or see someone you've met before, always introduce yourself again and mention your first name twice. "Hi, I'm Jane...Jane Smith. We met before. It's nice to see you again."

Chances are, the other person will respond with their name. Repeat the other person's name and make a comment about it in order to increase retention.

Tips to Remember Names

In networking situations, it's important to remember names. Yet many people complain as soon as they hear a name, it slips out of their mind. *Why?*

We have two types of memory: temporary and permanent. The temporary memory normally stores about seven items. The permanent memory holds information that must be retained. You can reinforce both the temporary and permanent memory by using controlled association, which links new incoming information to information already stored in your permanent memory.

In his book *Blueprints for Memory*, William D. Hersey offers specific exercises that can help you remember names and faces at networking and other events. In one exercise, Hersey suggests that you see a literal picture of the name, along with a visual image that captures whatever that name means to you. For the surname of Carpenter, for example, picture a woodworking tool in your mind's eye.

Smile

A smile is the universal symbol of positive energy and goodwill. A smile makes you approachable and puts others in a more positive frame of mind. Besides, the very act of smiling makes you feel happier and at ease.

Posture: Carry Yourself Like a Winner

Body language reveals more than the words we say. How straight we stand reveals how we see ourselves in relation to others.

Eye Contact Builds Trust

Making eye contact while you speak to people creates a strong emotional bond.

Keep in Contact via Touch Marketing

Experts say it takes seven impressions, or points of contact, for people to remember you. That's why sending an article or other information after meeting someone at a networking event is so powerful.

Nancy Michaels, marketing expert and author of *Perfecting Your Pitch*, makes herself memorable by sending contacts a card twice a year at unusual times—the Fourth of July and the Chinese New Year.

Ask yourself what you can do to keep in touch with your target audience at least seven times a year. Some ideas include:

> ➤ Print newsletters, electronic newsletters, and personal cards.

> ➤ A postcard campaign.

> ➤ Inexpensive holiday gifts.

> ➤ Free Internet downloads of valuable material from your Website.

> ➤ A free teleclass.

> ➤ E-mailing articles or links of interest.

Chapter Summary

1. Life is a series of sales presentations.

2. Networking is relationship building (not selling).

3. Networking should become a way of life.

4. Effective listening is the most important skill in your networking arsenal.

5. Projecting a professional image is essential for networking success.

6. Brainstorm your objective for attending an event in advance.

7. Attending networking events is a good way to meet people of influence.

8. Smiling telegraphs the fact you are friendly and approachable.

9. Dress how you wish to be perceived.

10. Keep conversations at networking events under six minutes.

11. Learning how to remember names is an important skill.

12. Make yourself memorable by sending articles the other person will find of interest.

Chapter Assignments

☐ Consider the image you want to project at a networking event and find the right outfit to support it.

☐ Write out your goals for the next three to six months, figure out the kind of people you need in order to meet those goals, and find networking groups that attract these kinds of people.

☐ Before every networking event, decide what you wish to accomplish.

☐ Train yourself to follow up with contacts. Add their business cards to your contact management database and find a way to keep in touch.

☐ Before events, try to get a sense of who will be there and who you want to meet. Ask the membership chairman for help introducing you to key people.

7

How Writing a Book Can Build Buzz, Brand, and Business

We are cups, constantly and
quietly being filled.
The trick is, knowing how
to tip ourselves over and
let the beautiful stuff out.
—Ray Bradbury, Author and
Creative Visionary
(b. 1920)

A fistful of years ago, John Fuhrman was yet another name-less sales trainer trapped in the 9-to-5 corporate world. One day, lightning flashed! *He would write a book!* Within months, *Reject Me—I Love It!* became a No. 1 best-seller, first giving him distinction and elevation above other sales trainers, then the financial and psychological resources to become lord and master of his own speaking/writing empire.

As a vehicle for building buzz for your business, a book underscores your credibility and serves as the best sales and marketing tool you can find. Books are a physical manifestation of your knowledge and expertise, inviting prospects, clients, and colleagues to understand your brilliance at a glance. Best yet, the convenient, portable format of a book organizes your intelligence, ideas, philosophy, and personality into one convenient, neatly sealed package.

In this chapter, we are going to explore the world of publishing and how it can help you generate credibility, media attention, and turn prospects into clients. We will also delve into the variety of publishing options available to you today, including traditional publishing, conventional self-publishing, and the new Print-On-Demand (POD) services offered by Internet-based publishing services. Finally, you will also learn systematic ways to outline and write your book, even if you have never written a word before.

Luring Media Attention—With Your Book as Bait!

Journalists are eager to write about your business. They need to use anecdotes of real people such as yourself to bring their stories to life. Yet their mantra is "trust, but verify" because sharp-eyed editors and hawk-nosed fact-checkers will go over whatever source they choose to use with a fine-toothed comb. Given a choice of choosing an expert to quote, journalists prefer to quote a source who has authored a book for added credibility.

Books as the Basis for Media Parties and Magnet Events

Parlay your forthcoming social swirl of book signings into a publicity machine in itself.

Author Debbi Karpowicz invited shoe manufacturer Allen-Edmonds to sponsor her marketing and publicity plan for her humorous dating book *I Love Men in Tasseled Loafers*, which included a flurry of outrageously colorful book signing parties with shoe-themed drinks (the "Tasseled Loafer") and music ("Blue Suede Shoes" and "Footloose").

As a result, the book was covered in more than 100 print and broadcast media outlets, which brought her notoriety, fame within her industry, and established her new niche as a savvy marketing expert.

Books as Tools of Transformation

Publishing a book can build or transform your business, tightly brand your niche, and position you as the expert of choice.

"A book brings your credibility to a whole new level," says Mary Lou Andre, a New England-based wardrobe consultant and the author of the top-selling *Ready to Wear*. "When seminar attendees find a book on their seat, they can't wait to hear you speak."

Nancy Michaels, author of *Perfecting Your Pitch*, considers a book an essential calling card: "Once you become a published author, the perception people have of you is elevated. Suddenly you have the authority behind you to work with larger clients, appear on television, and speak to larger audiences."

Books to Establish Niche and Brand

Authoring a book can help you create instant brand recognition and carve out a niche in a competitive field. Just a few years ago, Cindy Ventrice was one of thousands of consultant/ trainers who addressed a variety of management issues in the course of her practice.

One day, a reviewer from the respected San Francisco-based publisher Berrett-Koehler spotted an article she wrote for the American Society for Training & Development about employee recognition and asked her to submit a book proposal on the topic.

"I hadn't thought of writing a book, but took them up on the offer," explained Ventrice. "When the book was published, what I found was that it turned me into an expert on employee motivation. Now employee motivation and recognition is my niche field, and my brand."

Management consultant Margery Mayer uses her books on accountability to position herself in her niche, adding, "As a consultant, giving clients books is a personal gesture that solidifies relationships."

Fern Reiss self-published the five books in her *The Publishing Game* book series, which were quickly picked up as *Writer's Digest* Book Club selections. The series served to brand her as the go-to expert for book creation and product promotion. Even better, the books allowed her to develop a new platform for her high-priced, exclusive "Expertizing" seminars and paved the way for six-figure bids from traditional publishers for rights to her next book.

Like sardines in a can, Jack Canfield and Mark Victor Hansen were lumped together with a myriad of other motivational speakers before they published their original *Chicken Soup for the Soul*. The book quickly became a best-seller and turned them into name-brand motivational speakers (their very names are virtually synonymous with motivational speaking), branded a multimillion-dollar book series, and created a speaking and publishing empire with a myriad of spin-off products.

Reaching Your Niche Market

Gordon Burgett, author of more than 26 books and 1,700 articles, takes an upside-down approach to writing a book in that he first tests the market and then, if the report comes back favorably, writes the book.

Using this formula, he has created an empire around his books that feature speaking engagements, videos, cassettes, CDs, articles, and more. "If my targeted market will buy a book to meet a need or solve a problem, they will more likely buy something else to meet that need as well. What you are selling isn't just your book," he says, "but your expertise."

According to Burgett, a good niche market must:

> ❯ Have a vital need shared by all the members of the group.

> ❯ Have enough desire and income to seek and afford information to help them meet that need.

> ❯ Appear on an accessible, affordable, current, clean mailing list.

"If a group is registered and licensed, therefore it is listed and available," Burgett says, highlighting the importance of creating a marketing plan (here, consisting of the use of targeted mailing lists) even before beginning your book.

Books as News Pegs

John Boe, a sales trainer specializing in reading body language, was able to build buzz for his book and training services by piggybacking on the Kobe Bryant case. He wrote a news release with the headline: "The Truth About Lying: Deceitful Body Language That Kobe Bryant Couldn't Hide," which resulted in much media attention.

Traditional vs. Self-Publishing

After speaking engagements at conferences across the nation, people are so enthusiastic about authoring a book to build buzz for their business that they seek me out for more questions. Invariably, the question is this: "Should I find an agent and get traditionally published, go the self-publishing route, or go Print-On-Demand?"

The answer depends on the objectives of the individual and what he wants the book to accomplish.

Asked why he went with a traditional publisher, Lenny Laskowski, author of *10 Days to More Confident Public Speaking*, replied, "Going with a well-known publisher allowed me to elevate and justify my fees."

Cindy Ventrice went with Berrett-Koehler, knowing that a well-respected publisher would give her the enhanced credibility she needed to establish her niche.

Peter Bowerman, author of *The Well-Fed Writer*, was determined to self-publish from the get-go. He knew he had a ready market and thought self-publishing a book would be an excellent way to help folks learn how to make a successful business out of writing, while at the same time making more of a profit and keeping more control over the process.

Fern Reiss had a six-figure offer from a mainstream publisher to buy her first book, *The Infertility Diet*, but she was confident she could create enough buzz in this niche community to generate positive word of mouth and breakthrough sales on her own, so she decided to self-publish.

Debbie Allen self-published because she knew she had a great title in *Confessions of Shameless Self Promoters*. She also knew the book's potential, how to market it, and how to turn it into a media magnet.

Understanding the Print-On-Demand (POD) Process

What is the difference between traditional self-publishing and the printing process known as POD?

In conventional self-publishing, the author takes on the myriad of duties performed by traditional publishing houses. She writes the book, hires an editor, hires an interior and cover designer, hires a printer, engages a distributor, and markets and publicizes the book. The self-publisher is also responsible for purchasing a block of ISBN tracking numbers. After paying vendors for their services, the self-publisher keeps all profits.

By contrast, POD authors need only submit an electronic manuscript to the POD publisher and pay an up-front fee ranging from $400 to $1,000 for publication. The POD author then buys units of books back from the POD publisher at a discount.

Traditionally, authors have had little choice as to cover and interior design, but now many online POD publishers are adding options such as design, editing, and even publicity for an additional price.

The upside of POD is that you can create an "instant book" to use as a leave-behind for clients or sell in small quantities at the back of the room during speaking engagements. Previously published authors with out-of-print books can also use POD to get their books back in circulation and benefit from new income streams.

The downside of POD is that bookstores are hesitant to accept POD books and reviewers are reluctant to review them.

"POD is a viable option for professionals," says Jan Nathan, executive director of the Publishers Marketing Association, but emphasizes that POD is not a "publishing process," but rather a "printing process," and that authors need an editor, formatter, and cover artist to project true credibility.

Penny C. Sansevieri, a marketing and media relations specialist whose tag line is "turning authors into success stories," encourages business professionals to consider POD for several reasons. "First," explains Sansevieri, "authors retain their creative license. Traditional publishing houses can pull chapters and edit at will. When you use POD, you keep control. Second, you can have your book in print as quick as possible, perhaps within two weeks or less. With traditional publishing, the journey can take two years or more. Third, you can test market with POD inexpensively and efficiently."

To bring the last point home, Sansevieri explains that she first published *Get Published Today!* as a POD book in order to test the market. Because she was speaking in many adult centers, which included the price of the book in the course materials, she offered students a complimentary gift for filling out feedback forms. Sansevieri used the feedback to form the basis for her new revision, and advises that if anyone is interested in test marketing the potential for a traditionally published book, POD is a great place to start.

"Another way that people can use POD is to get testimonials," says Sansevieri. "Celebrities need to see an actual book with an ISBN number before they are willing to give a testimonial. Often authors will print a POD edition to get celebrity endorsements, and then contact publishers and say, 'These celebrities think this book is great, what about you?'"

Sansevieri presumes that the reason POD published books may have a perceived stigma is because the very first PODs could be considered "science experiments" in that authors underestimated the *value of editing* before having their manuscript printed in book form.

"Today, that stigma is fading. Explore your choices with POD today and you can find POD hardback editions and color interiors. The differences between self-publishing, traditional publishing, and POD are less distinguishable," says Sansevieri. "How you choose to publish is a personal decision. If you have the time and willingness that it takes to get traditionally published, go for it. If you do not want to wait, there is nothing wrong with POD or self-publishing as long as it does not 'look' self-published."

Carl Friesen, a management consultant and member of the Institute of Management Consultants, decided to go with Xlibris, a POD publisher.

"My objective in getting published was mostly to *get published*," says Friesen, who helps professionals get published in business magazines as part of their marketing. "I didn't want to take the time needed to deal with an agent, get a publisher, 'sell' my concept to them, and all that. It would have been too much of a diversion from my core practice. So, I spent the $1,200 needed to get my book on the Xlibris system. With the improvements in photo-based publishing, binding, and Internet-based fulfillment, self-publishing is a so much more viable option these days."

Friesen notes that he had first been published by a professional association as part of a "no-money" deal—they didn't pay for the manuscript, and he didn't get royalties. That manuscript formed the basis of the Xlibris book that was published the next year.

Thomas Plante, Ph.D., ABPP, psychology professor and director for the Center for Professional Development at Santa Clara University, has written seven books with academic and traditional publishers, including John Wiley & Sons, but used

Internet-based POD publisher AuthorHouse for his book *Getting Together and Staying Together: The Stanford University Course on Intimate Relationships*.

Why did he choose POD?

"I didn't have to suffer with quirky editors who had a vision of a book very different from my own. Neither did I have to endure endless reviews of the manuscript or have to satisfy the various whims of reviewers," Plante explains.

During the clergy sex abuse scandal, Plante recalls he was interviewed daily by CNN, *U.S. News & World Report*, and *TIME* as the author of *Bless Me Father for I Have Sinned*. ABCNews even shot a special hour report using the title of the book. But according to Plante, the media coverage did not result in massive sales because the book was priced by his academic publisher at $60, and when they ran out of copies, it took several months to print more. "If it could be downloaded for a few dollars, or available as a POD book, more people would have access to the information."

As you have seen, there are a myriad of ways and reasons to publish a book. Yet professionals often ask how they can measure their return on investment, as writing any book— whether traditionally published, POD, or conventionally self-published—takes time that may be better spent with clients.

Judith Appelbaum, head of Sensible Solutions, a marketing firm that helps publishers reach their niche market, offers a no-nonsense perspective on this topic: "If you are looking at a book as a way to make money directly, you should probably pick another project. Most books aren't profitable with that calculation. But if you look at a book as a calling card, a promotional device, a way to get ideas out there, change the world and draw in more clients, then the calculation changes. Provided that the book is good and well-marketed, you can expect it to pay off, but the payoff will come indirectly in the form of new business from new clients and from current and former clients. So if you are an expensive consultant or professional, the question to ask about money is not 'How many copies will I have to sell to recoup my investment?' but 'How many new assignments do I need to pay for the books?'"

The Writing Process: Getting Started

Now that we've covered the pros and cons of choosing a printing method, let's move forward and focus on content. Sitting in front of a computer and keyboard for the first time, facing a blank screen, many professionals panic. *How do I write this thing? How do I even start?*

Many writers eagerly dash off the first 50 pages in a burst of inspiration. Reading over their pages, they begin to rewrite. And rewrite. Ultimately, they never finish the first chapter because frustration sets in when the words on the page don't seem to live up to their expectations.

When you write a non-fiction book, structure and pre-planning are everything. You might have heard the phrase "writing is rewriting." It's natural to expect our first efforts to read like a finely edited work. You will soon discover that your first job is to simply get your content material on the page. Next, organize your material, give it life and color, and then begin the perfection process.

Beginning With Back Cover Copy

Self-publishing guru Dan Poynter suggests that before anything else, you create the back cover copy in your mind and on paper to help you focus. Concisely state what the book is about and what the reader will gain by reading your book.

Create compelling marketing copy and bullet points that promise strong benefits such as health, wealth, entertainment, or a better life. Promise to make readers better at what they do. Look at the back covers from books on your own bookshelf to give you inspiration, and try it yourself.

Beginning With a Sales Letter

Ken Winston Caine, former Rodale editor, suggests that before you write the table of contents, you write a sales letter to yourself to bring home the exciting benefits the book will offer the reader. Note that a sales letter is written in personal, from-me-to-you language.

Caine's approach is great for summoning enthusiasm and excitement for your writing project. Many of us do not consider ourselves "natural salesmen" and too many of us have issues or blocks about promoting ourselves and our ideas. Here is his technique for jump-starting a book:

Writing the Sales Letter

by Ken Winston Caine

Before writing a word of your book, write the hottest sales letter that you can imagine for your book. Pull all stops. Throw in every wild promise that comes to mind. Promise everything you would ever hope to get…if you were buying or reading such a book. And then some.

And sell it. Sell hard. Tell me why I need this book and exactly every single way that it is going to change my life for the better.

A good sales letter is at least 12 pages long. So you've got room to write. Go to it.

Include all the lists of things I am going to find in the book. That is, the seven secrets to XYZ. The never-fail formula for XYZ. The three words every successful XYZ utters every morning while reaching for the toothpaste. On and on.

When you have written an utterly compelling sales letter describing the ultimate dream book on your subject, then…write the book. Write the book and fulfill all the promises of the sales letter. (Well, most of them. Some just won't pan. And so, in the end, you'll revise the sales letter a bit to reflect the finished book—if you're going to actually use it as a sales letter. And why not?)

Writing a full-blown sales letter for your book before you begin writing or even outlining your book, and using the sales letter as a blueprint for the book, really helps you think in terms of how it will benefit your readers.

© Ken Winston Caine

Creating an "About the Author"

Begin *now* to assemble information about yourself that you can use in your proposal to impress agents and editors. Sometimes, the "About the Author" section is the first place agents and editors turn to when they are considering a proposal.

Increasingly, agents are demanding that authors have a national platform before even reading their proposal. They are looking for authors who have name recognition, write articles, and are active on the speaking circuit. Authors with national platforms are easier to sell and market.

It's important to create an electronic and physical file for all of your accomplishments. A long laundry list of impressive speaking engagements; letters of recommendation from delighted, well-known companies and clients; media appearances; article placements; and active involvement or honorary roles in prestigious associations can go a long way in selling yourself and your work.

The Book Proposal

You will find three excellent books on proposal writing in the resources section at the end of this book, but for now, realize that the basic elements of a book proposal are as follows:

> The concept statement.

> About the book.

> About the author.

> About the market.

> About the competition.

> Table of contents.

> Chapter summaries.

> Sample chapters.

Writing the Proposal

Your first step is to write a book proposal, even if you plan on conventional self-publishing or POD. Going through the formal process of a proposal will help you discover your book idea's strengths, potential areas of weakness, and how strongly it can stand out against the competition.

First, ask yourself, "Who is my market?" Figure out who your target audience is, and their specific needs and wants. What is their challenge? How can your book help them solve this challenge? Begin with the end in mind. Clearly visualize who will buy your book, and the solutions and benefits they expect as a result of reading it.

Next, analyze your competition. *What books are competing against the one you are proposing? How is your book different or better?*

Identifying your competition early on can help you give your book a unique slant, as well as further niche and shape your book. Although the process of writing a proposal may seem laborious, by writing out your table of contents and chapter summaries, the actual writing of your book will be as simple as writing by numbers.

What Agents and Editors Look for in a Proposal

Paula Munier, director of product development at Adams Media, says this about what she wants to see in a proposal: "I want to see that the idea is well-conceived and that the author can execute the book. I want to see a chapter-by-chapter outline, the author addressing why he is the right person to write the book. I want to sense the author is as interested in the book's success as I am. Finally, authors should be familiar with our list and prepared to explain why the book is good for our list."

Colleen Mohyde, literary agent and partner in the Doe Coover agency in Massachusetts, describes a proposal as "a unique hybrid type of writing." "On one hand," Mohyde says, "it demonstrates your writing skills. On the other, it is a sales tool. A proposal is a form of courtship. You are wooing the editor, putting your best foot forward, making a terrific first impression with the promise of something more to come. A writer needs to demonstrate in the proposal that she is bursting with enough ideas to fill a book and give evidence of some solid ones, with the tease that this is just the tip of the iceberg."

Query Letters: The First Step in Submitting Proposals

With your book proposal reworked to perfection, it is time to send it off into the world. But wait! Do not actually send your proposal. Send a query letter explaining what your proposal is about to ascertain interest.

By now, you are probably wondering if you should send your proposal to an agent or an editor at a publishing house. According to Michael Larsen of the Larsen-Pomada Agency, here are a few key reasons why you need an agent:

1. Agents can approach editors at major houses who won't consider work from unrepresented writers.

2. Agents know which editors and publishers to submit to and, just as important, which to avoid.

3. Agents keep as many subsidiary rights (movies, foreign rights, ect.) as possible for their authors. This means the authors will make more money from these rights, receiving it sooner than if a publisher keeps them.

Colleen Mohyde, literary agent and partner at the Doe Coover agency, says:

> "An agent is the writer's advocate through the entire process, and the publishing teacher, too, helping you translate and understand a very subjective, taste-driven business.

> "Editors at the major houses prefer to acquire books through agents, as they get a project with a 'seal of approval.' Another publishing professional has already screened the work for the editor. Editors also prefer to negotiate a sale of a book through an agent as they speak the same language and the process is streamlined."

Judith Appelbaum, head of Sensible Solutions, suggests that experts send queries first and then proposals directly to editors for a variety of reasons, including the fact that there are many more editors than agents. The secret, Appelbaum says, is to carefully research the market for your book and choose the editors who will be most receptive. One way to find editors is by making a list of books that are similar in some significant way to the book you plan to write and checking the acknowledgments pages. If an editor's name isn't in the book, she adds, you can often get it by calling the publisher or by doing some research on the Internet.

Both approaches can work, and the key element to take from Appelbaum's comment is that the more research you do, on both the agent and the editor, the more success you will enjoy. You need to focus on agents and editors who have demonstrated interest in the material with which you are presenting them. Appelbaum wishes to make it clear to prospective authors that they should not approach agents and editors at the same time. You have to target one or the other within a given period.

How to Write a Query Letter

Appelbaum offers these tips for strong, focused queries, adapted from her book *How to Get Happily Published*:

The "How to Get Happily Published" Query Checklist

by Judith Appelbaum

The best way to approach editors is with a good solid, interesting "query"—i.e., a one-page letter that asks, in effect, for an invitation to present your book proposal.

The query should:

▶ Address an individual editor by name and explain why you believe that particular editor will be interested in the book you're trying to place.

▶ State your specific idea (as opposed to your general subject) and offer a catchy, informative working title.

▶ Describe the main point your manuscript makes, the ground it covers, and its style.

▶ Present a very brief excerpt by way of illustration.

▶ Explain where and how you got (or are getting) your material.

▶ Mention your relevant connections and qualifications.

▶ Show how what you have to say is fresh and different from specific articles and/or books now in print.

▶ Estimate the length of your finished manuscript and propose a delivery date.

▶ Convey a strong sense of enthusiasm.

Good queries to appropriate editors get responses that say, "Yes, your work interests me, please send it along."

Conventional Letter vs. E-mail Query

Recently, the *Wall Street Journal* (*WSJ*) published a story titled "Book Idea in an E-mail Box," which discussed the wisdom of sending an e-mail pitch. As of 2004, most agents and editors admit to trashing e-mail queries, but a growing number seem to be receptive.

The *WSJ* cited the success story of Susan Farren, a stay-at-home mother of five in California who sent an e-mail query to Hyperion with the words "Fireman's Wife" in the subject line. Editor-in-Chief Will Schwalbe opened the e-mail, assuming it concerned another book he had edited. But after reading the pitch, he was hooked, and the author got her deal.

The *WSJ* article also mentioned Gini Graham Scott, who offers a query writing service called PublishersAndAgents.net. When Scott sent out her own e-mail pitch to editors, "Do You Look Like Your Dog" it sold within two weeks.

My best advice is to call the agency before you send your query and ask the receptionist the preferred method of transmission.

Getting Contact Information for Publishers and Agents

As various experts quoted in this book stressed, personal connections are key. Don't be afraid to bring up a time you met an agent or publisher at a conference, or even bought a conference tape and were impressed by their words of wisdom. Peek into the acknowledgment sections of books similar to yours to see which agents are being thanked by their authors. Read the gossipy "Big Deals" section of *Publishers Weekly* to see agents who are selling books like yours for big bucks.

Also, visit your library and peruse the many fine directories for finding publishers, such as *Literary Marketplace*; *Publishers, Distributors & Wholesalers of the United States*; and *Writer's Market*.

Alternatives to Agents

Finding a publisher on your own is sometimes more promising than enticing an agent. It is possible to find individuals in the publishing world who work on a fixed fee to act as an agent, such as Ken Lizotte, chief imaginative officer of Emerson Consulting Group, Inc. According to Lizotte, the advantage to his service is that while most agents will give up when a manuscript fails to sell quickly, he will keep pushing because he is not commission-based, and it is critical that he delivers real results in order to justify his fee.

Constructing Your Book: Tips From the Masters

Every author begins the writing process in a unique way. Over the years, I've followed methods offered by self-publishing guru Dan Poynter and former Rodale editor Ken Winston Caine with much success.

The Dan Poynter Approach

Dan Poynter, author of *The Self-Publishing Manual*, is a pioneer, living legend, and major force in shaping the self-publishing industry into what it is today. He has launched the books and transformed the careers of thousands of authors who have read his books, attended his programs, and followed his methods to publishing success.

Poynter advises authors to begin shaping their material with the "pilot system," in which they start by drawing up a preliminary table of contents (10–12 chapters), then sort their research material (including photocopied material) into the appropriate chapter files. "Pick up an interesting pile," Poynter says, "and go through it, underlining important points and writing in additional comments. Write out longer thoughts on a separate piece of paper and file them to order in the pile."

According to Poynter, this "floor spread" will allow you to see the whole interrelated project, lending excitement and encouragement. He advises moving the piles around to ensure a good, logical flow of thought.

Poynter also advocates keeping a notebook with you at all times: "When a particularly original thought or creative approach hits you, write it down or you will lose it. Keep on thinking and keep on note-taking. Add your thoughts and major pieces to the piles. As you go along, draw up a list of questions as they come to mind so that you will remember to follow up on them for answers."

"Strip your notes by cutting, sorting, and taping," Poynter advises. "Paste the strips together with Magic transparent tape. Write on the tape and the paper when adding notes. Then dictate from the pasted strips. Write as you speak; relax and be clear. Your objective is to get your thoughts and research material onto the hard disk. Make notes where you are considering illustrations."

On any writing project, momentum is key. Poynter suggests leaving the first chapter for the end. Instead, select the chapter pile that looks the smallest, easiest, or most fun. If you lack a certain piece of information, a number or a fact, leave a blank space, put a note in the text to remind you, and go on—do not lose momentum! Once you have drafted it, take the next most interesting chapter, and soon you will be past the halfway mark. You will be encouraged and gather momentum. Now, it's time to write the first chapter, as it's usually introductory in nature and you cannot know where you are going until you have been there. Many authors wind up rewriting and giving the chapter a new slant because they wrote it first.

Review each chapter in order and, if possible, give yourself a two-week period to shut out all distractions and become totally involved in the manuscript. As a result, there will be greater continuity, less duplication, and clearer organization.

The Ken Winston Caine Approach

Ken Winston Caine offers the following approach to writing and shaping your book:

_____

_____

Writing the Table of Contents and Shaping the Book
by Ken Winston Caine

It helps up front, especially with non-fiction, to figure out the 20 most significant things you want to say. Word each enticingly. Those are your 20 chapters. I put them on index cards and shuffle them around until they are in the right order.

Then, for each chapter, what are 15 or so essential points or twists? That's how I outline these days. My table of contents (and each chapter's subpoints) is my outline. I also tend to write the subpoints on index cards. One card for each. And shuffle them around until I have a good order, where one point leads to the next or builds on the previous. Word the points in exciting, intriguing, promising language. That makes the writing more fun and helps you keep up the tone and enthusiasm.

If you can put together a table of contents of that nature, you'll do a tremendous lot of selling and organizing up front. And once you start writing, you'll never be at a loss for what to write next. Each chapter should be roughly 10 pages long. So on average, each of the 15 points in the chapter gets about 2/3 of a page. That's the popular, non-fiction book formula, and is a style that editors and agents are comfortable with.

Spend as long as it takes to get the table of contents so it feels right to you. So that it's hot. So that anyone in your target audience who even glances at the table of contents is going to exclaim, "I've *got* to read this book."

Then just write like hell, and never look back until you type the words, "The End."

A convenient way I break my own rule, is to keep a journal alongside the computer as I write. And I jot in it, immediately, as my mind sees diversions and different approaches to a chapter, different ways to order chapters, etc. I jot in it what I am seeing and how I might rewrite, rework later, who I might call and interview as a source, etc. And then I don't read that journal until I am ready to rewrite. Or, more truthfully, until I am finished writing for the day. Then I *am* likely to quickly look at my notes—especially if I had a great flash on how to reorganize upcoming chapters. I may incorporate that change in progress if it's easy to do and seems especially logical and helpful.

Another way to keep the manuscript moving is to leave blanks in places where you know you need to flesh out some more. I use a couple lines of *X*s and then write a brief note of what is needed there (fact, story, source…etc.). Follow that with a couple lines of Xs. Those holes then are easy to spot and fill at rewrite time.

I've been coaching writers for 30 years, and the most common problem I find those tackling their first book projects encounter is the tendency to edit themselves and keep rewriting the first 10 pages. Or first 100 pages. Or to keep rewriting each page as it comes out, trying to perfect it. Plenty of time for that later. Spin the *whole* thing out first. It will go much faster. And the faster you go, truly, the better it will flow. The less likely you are to bog it down in techno-language, and complicated sentences, and 50-dollar words, and complex thinking.

My biggest single piece of advice to any writer is: *just write the thing*. Whip out a first draft as fast and furiously as you can. Don't do a single paragraph of rewriting until the entire first draft is done. Then let it sit for a week, read it with notepad in hand, and make a million notes on how to improve it, reorganize it, reword it. And go to work on the rewrite.

Once you're happy with the rewrite, solicit 10 to 30 readers. These are friends, acquaintances, even experts in the field, who agree to read your draft and critique, comment on it, and especially to note anything they stumbled on, found confusing, difficult to get through, grasp, offensive, etc.

They (like an R and D team) are expected to produce their comments on a certain deadline. (A few will never turn in their comments.)

Read the comments. Consider them. Do some more rewriting.

© Ken Winston Caine

The Ross's Approach

Here is one more method using note cards, culled from Tom and Marilyn Ross's excellent book, *The Complete Guide to Self-Publishing*. They begin the book creation process on the floor with a handful of 3 × 5-inch cards labeled with possible subject areas. They sort through their ideas and research material like a deck of cards, dealing them out to the various subject areas fanned around them alphabetically. Once the cards are in their appropriate stack, they look for common denominators. When these patterns begin to emerge, they can understand the best way to order them, and the book's skeleton begins to take shape.

How to Balance Writing and Taking Care of Your Business

Another question many professionals pose at conferences is how they can justify taking time away from their business to write a book, and if they would be able to measure their return on investment.

Cindy Ventrice, who kept her business thriving by writing between 4 a.m. and 8 a.m., answers the question this way:

"If someone wants to write a book thinking that royalties will pay for the time it takes to write and market it, don't bother. But if what they are looking for is something that heightens their credibility and leads to more work, better work, higher paying work, it's the right approach."

Following are three techniques you can use to keep your business in the black while writing a book:

#1: Consider a Ghostwriter

If you simply can't take the time to write the book that can take you to the next professional level, you may want to consider a ghostwriter. Your skill is in your area of expertise, which may not include the art of translating the brilliance of your ideas into the written word. Often, a professional in this area can express your essence and platform better than you can yourself (ghostwriters can be hired just to write the proposal, not the whole book). This way, you can shop your idea in proposal form, sell it, and, if you want to have the entire book ghostwritten, use your advance to pay the ghostwriter. Unless you are a celebrity, you most likely won't be able to sell your idea in a pitch or letter. You will need a proposal. Consider hiring a ghostwriter to put the chain in motion by writing your proposal.

In addition to writing skills, a good ghostwriter brings experience to the project. They've "been there and done that" with many experts before you, so they have a natural feel for how to shape your material.

Robin Quinn, a ghostwriter based in Southern California, has been generous enough to create a list of what experts should be aware of when considering a ghostwriter.

Tips for Hiring a Ghostwriter

▸ Look at samples of a ghostwriter's earlier writing to see if it meets the quality and feeling you are going for.

▸ Look for honesty in your initial meeting. The ghostwriter should tell you whether there is potential in you or an idea. An ethical ghostwriter is not going to encourage you to invest in a book that has little promise of success.

▸ Skilled ghostwriters can offer suggestions if they feel a change of approach will improve the book's chances. Ghostwriters often will lay out the structure of the book, reflected in a table of contents.

▸ Research. In many cases involving experts looking to write a book, most of the background and information comes from them. This is essentially why *they* are considered the authors. Experts usually have spent a lot of time developing their concept and amassing information and ideas. The ghostwriter is simply the *channel*—the one who creates the words that will most effectively convey the message. In my ghost projects so far, I have done supplementary research and further development of the ideas, but some ghostwriters do not consider that their job. Research is definitely a point to be covered early in your discussions.

▸ Credit. In ghostwriting, the range for the credit of the book goes from no acknowledgment at all (not the way to go, in my opinion), to a "thank you" in the acknowledgments, to a "with" or "as told to" credit on the cover, to a full co-author line on the cover. Some people argue that a writer who receives a co-author line is a co-author, not a ghost. However, if the "co-author" actually wrote the entire book, wasn't some ghosting involved? You should work out the best arrangement for your particular project.

▸ Money. Here the range is considerable. Some ghosts are willing to postpone payment in exchange for royalties, which may turn out to be minimal. On the other end of the spectrum, in rare situations, writers who ghost celebrity books can make more than

$100,000 per book. A ghost may estimate an overall project fee or prefer to work at an hourly rate. In either case, a share of royalties can also be part of the agreement, and reimbursement of the ghost's expenses for phone, express delivery, etc., is usually covered. Again, you should negotiate for whatever suits a given project best.

© Robin Quinn

What about confidentiality?

Quinn answers the question this way. "As with any relationship, a cooperative attitude and shared enthusiasm will help push the project forward to completion. A professional ghostwriter is discreet and does not intrude on the author's role once the book goes into publication. I am available for questions from my clients, but stay mostly ghostly invisible once the book is in print. In turn, my authors understand the need for referrals and recommendations. On that last note, a good way to track down those phantom ghostwriters with proven skills is by asking your colleagues for recommendations."

#2: Ask Experts to Write Chapters for Your Book

Debbie Allen, author of *Confessions of Shameless Self Promoters*, was too busy with her speaking business to put aside time to write an entire book. She brainstormed a great title and marketing plan, then reached out to established, well-known experts in the self-promotion niche. Allen sent them a detailed marketing proposal for the book and a letter asking them to contribute a few pages to make up a chapter. Because these established experts could see from her detailed marketing proposal that by contributing to Allen's book they would further their own publicity, they agreed.

#3: Offer a Chapter in a Joint Publishing Effort

A growing number of companies are putting together books made up of individual chapters by noted experts in their field. Depending on the company, a spokesperson will either interview the author over the phone or accept a chapter based on articles or speeches the author has written or delivered. Authors are expected to buy a predetermined amount of copies in advance.

Alternatives to Books

Is there an alternative to the time, energy, and expense of writing a book that works to underscore your credibility and can be sent to prospects as a low-cost, value-added representation of your services?

The answer is yes. It is called a booklet.

A booklet is between 16 and 24 pages and educates its target audience with tips, techniques, or strategies. They range from 3,000 and 5,000 words and can be printed or made available online.

You can also create a tip-oriented booklet for each concept or issue you cover in your consulting or professional practice.

Paulette Ensign, a speaker/consultant on the production and uses of booklets, underscores the fact that booklets are excellent promotional tools for your book or business, as you can license the content of your booklets to large corporations who can distribute it to thousands of employees or tens of thousands of customers in dozens of languages, thus getting you heightened visibility.

As you now know, there is a multitude of ways to write and sell your book. The key decision that you must make is not how, but when, you will begin.

Chapter Summary

1. Authoring a book can transform your professional life and take it to exciting new levels.

2. Books are an excellent news peg to highlight other areas of your business.

3. Books can position you as the "go to" expert in your field.

4. Books can help you establish niche and brand.

5. You have the freedom to choose between a variety of publishing methods to suit your budget and objectives.

6. Determine to write a proposal, even if you are planning to self-publish or use Print-On-Demand (POD).

7. Begin the writing process with a "sales letter," in which you promise the reader everything you would hope to get yourself if you were buying the book.

8. Write the table of contents by organizing like information in various physical piles or on-screen lists.

9. Keep your clients and/or day job by writing two to four hours a day before work.

10. Consider a ghostwriter if your schedule does not allow you to take time off to write.

11. Submit a query letter to editors or agents first, describing your proposal and asking if they want to see it.

12. Booklets are a viable alternative to books for consultants who want a way to establish their expertise in physical form.

Chapter Assignments

☐ Begin to observe TV, radio, and print interviews with authors, especially authors in a field similar to yours. Attune to the way they deliver their book's message. Envision yourself talking to Matt Lauer about your own book. Visualize it clearly and often.

☐ Invest in a notebook and begin to write down the many ways you can see yourself using the book once it is published. Would you give it to clients in order to get an edge over the competition?

☐ If you are leaning toward self-publishing, investigate discussion groups on the Internet and actively ask questions. Seek advice. You will find people are generous with hard-to-find information online.

☐ Begin constructing an "About Me" file and add to it daily. Vow to write at least one line a day about a new accomplishment or a way that you and your book are unique. This will come in handy in the "About the Author" section of your proposal.

☐ One day, grab a bunch of your favorite books from your bookshelf. Turn them so that you see the back cover instead of the front. Notice how the copywriter created strong headlines and promised irresistible benefits. Write down the phrasing of the headlines and benefits that strike an emotional chord.

8

How to Build Buzz With Public Speaking

Grasp the subject, the words
will follow.
—Cato the Elder,
Roman Orator
(234 B.C.–149 B.C.)

"**N**o one ever really noticed me," an entrepreneur and fellow member of the National Speakers Association tells me, "until I began to speak at the major conferences, and also to groups in my city. Now everyone is rushing up to me, exclaiming, 'I see your name everywhere!'"

One of the major advantages of public speaking is knowing that thousands of others in your industry, along with potential clients, will see your name and picture on postcards, in glossy conference brochures, in the newspaper, and on the Internet.

Why is public speaking such a great promotional tool? When you speak, you are perceived as an expert and establish immediate credibility with the audience, many of whom may engage you for private consultation.

Public speaking can be used to build your business in a multitude of ways. It creates top of the mind awareness of your services in the mind of your target market, it helps colleagues think of you and generate referrals, it gets you free publicity, and it goes a long way to establishing your authority as the expert of choice.

If you have never spoken before, start small. Consider joining Toastmasters, a supportive organization for beginning and advanced speakers that gives you the opportunity to practice speaking in a supportive environment. Or, give a class at your local adult center, college, or religious organization. You will soon gain the confidence you need to speak to your peers on a professional level.

Speaking for Many Reasons

What do you want to accomplish as a result of your speaking? Possibilities include enhanced publicity, picking up new clients, adding prospects to your e-mail list, reaching new markets, selling products, giving back to the community, and more.

Some people use public speaking as a way to test the market for a new book or product or to refine the development of a book in progress. Penny C. Sansevieri gives talks related to publishing and used her class at the San Diego Learning Annex to refine the manuscript that turned out to be her book *Get Published Today!*

Diane Darling, CEO of Effective Networking, Inc., and author of *The Networking Survival Guide*, likes to speak at the Los Angeles Learning Annex because her picture, company name, and copies of her book jacket go out to the Learning

Annex's mailing list of more than 100,000 and are offered free in hundreds of locations around the city. "It's the best form of free advertising you can get," Darling says.

Ken Lizotte, chief imaginative officer of Emerson Consulting Group, Inc., speaks before a variety of associations as members are in the position to use his article writing and book development services.

Finding Speaking Opportunities

Speaking opportunities are all around you. Just look in the "Calendar" section of your local business journal and city newspaper to see the various events hosted by local chapters of national associations, business and civic organizations, etc., in addition to speaking at continuing adult education centers. Also, check your mail, e-mail, and trade association publications for announcements of industry meetings and conventions.

Your local library should have a copy of the *Encyclopedia of Associations*, which gives a full listing of all associations, including contact information. Find those within your niche and ask them directly about their need for speakers at conventions and local chapters, as well as asking to be included on their mailing list.

Contacting Associations

When you find an association or other organization who uses speakers similar to yourself, find out who is in charge of program development. Frequently, this is not a staff position, but rather a volunteer effort by a board member. Introduce yourself, ask about their programs and conferences, and, if you can, submit a proposal.

Writing Articles to Generate Conference Speaking Events

Many associations within your target market have print and online newsletters and are always in need of quality content. Writing articles for association newsletters (either for free or a fee) is a great way to increase awareness and get booked as a speaker.

After a few of your articles have appeared, contact the VP of programming, say you've received good feedback on your articles and that you would like to give more value by delivering a presentation at their next conference. Continue to write articles before the presentation to increase name recognition, and, afterwards, to help retention of your key points.

Elements of a Successful Proposal

Whether you are pitching the director of an adult education center such as the Learning Annex, a meeting planner, or the program director of a conference, offer to send a proposal that includes:

> A catchy seminar title.

> Descriptive customized marketing copy for your talk.

> Your bio.

> Your picture.

> Testimonials.

> Bulleted key learning points of your talk.

> Expected outcomes.

> A partial list of where you have spoken before.

> A handout or other supporting material.

> An audio CD or video from a similar presentation you gave.

Customizing Your Talk

Many people speak on topics of key interest to their target market, but tweak their presentations to even more closely match the specific interest of the audience they will be addressing. Consider making things easy on yourself by creating a template of your proposals that you keep on your computer or in your journal so you can shoot off a proposal in an instant.

For example, my basic talks are on public relations and enhancing presentation skills. Whether I'm addressing the needs of accountants, authors, or management consultants, the basic structure of my talk is the same, but in the proposal stage I customize the selling copy of the talk to match the pressing needs of that industry.

Let's say I was addressing the Publishers Marketing Association at their annual conference. I'd snoop around the Internet to find shocking new statistics or trends and build a hook, similar to the way you have learned to build a hook for your PR news.

In this scenario, one interesting fact I might uncover is that according to Bowker's Books in Print database (*www.booksinprint.com*), the U.S. title output in 2003 increased a staggering 19 percent to 175,000 new titles and editions—the highest total ever recorded. This means that 478 books come out each day—a sobering statistic that would motivate an author to realize the importance of taking responsibility for their own publicity.

How to Create Eye-Catching Titles That Entice Attendees

According to advertising guru David Ogilvy, 97 percent of the population glances at a headline or title without reading the copy that follows. The best seminar titles promise great benefits, yet are short, snappy, and often rhyme. Here are some ideas to get you started:

1. **Fill in the blanks titles.**

   For example:

   "How to _____ So You Can _____."

2. **Titles using alliteration.**

   Think along the lines of the best-selling book titled *The Power of Positive Thinking*.

3. **Titles with funny sounds.**

   Scientists have discovered that the human ear perks up at certain sounds. Words with the letter *K* are included. Comedians have long learned that some words, such as pickle, are funnier than others. Consider a title like "Fashion Chic Meets Techno Geek."

4. **Titles that rhyme.**

   A good example is the title "Twinges in Your Hinges?" to describe a talk given by orthopedic surgical nurse Linda Brown. (You can find help with rhymes at *www.rhymezone.com*.)

5. **Titles using chiaroscuro.**

   A painting with contrast between black and white is called *chiaroscuro*. Try this technique with your seminar title, borrowing from titles such as "The Rise and Fall" and "The Agony and the Ecstasy."

Create Your Own Speaking and Seminar Opportunities

You can also create your own speaking opportunities by setting up your own seminar.

Fern Reiss, CEO of Expertizing.com, has built prestige and profits by creating "Expertizing" workshops, which she runs at Ritz-Carlton hotels in Manhattan, Boston, and Washington, D.C. In the workshops, she trains participants to achieve fame for their expertise and media attention for their business.

"Basically, people take this workshop because they're interested in achieving the same kind of media attention I've gotten," says Reiss, who has been quoted in more than 100 prestigious publications, including the *New York Times* and the *Wall Street Journal*.

Reiss distributes her "Expertizing" workshop flyer at national workshops, conferences, and corporate talks across the country. Because the "Expertizing" workshop fee is $2,500 and limited to just 10 participants, Reiss only needs to attract one or two attendees from each forum to fill her workshops.

"The advantage of doing a high-priced workshop is that it's actually easier to fill, because you have fewer seats to sell, and the cachet factor actually helps," adds Reiss, who does no advertising and only announces upcoming workshops at her speaking gigs and through occasional mailings to her growing e-mail list.

Bob Norton, president of C-Level Enterprises, Inc., launched his CEO and Entrepreneur Boot Camp in 2004 titled "The Art and Science of Business Design."

The following are his tips for setting up your own seminar.

Tips for Creating Your Own Seminar

1. Ask yourself how you are going to get your mailing list for your seminar in a way that is targeted and cost-effective.

    Advertising and marketing costs can total many hundreds of dollars for a single seat if you go through direct mail and traditional marketing vehicles. Instead, find appropriate partnerships and trade permission-based, opt-in lists to drive marketing and acquisition costs down.

2. Understand that a lucrative "back end" may justify breaking even, or even losing money on a seminar.

    Back of the room sales and attracting clients for long-term consulting can be more lucrative than tuition.

3. When conceiving your seminar idea, build product ideas into the mix.

    Get your program videotaped and audiotaped in a way that makes sense so that you have an ongoing revenue stream.

© Bob Norton

Publicizing Your Seminar

Regardless of whether you are producing your own seminar or you are giving a talk for an association or other organization who will be doing the publicity, it's a smart idea to build buzz for the seminar yourself. Even if it is an out-of-town seminar and local prospects and colleagues can't attend, be certain everyone knows about it.

Here are some quick ways to get the word out:

> ❯ An independent "news blast" to your e-zine subscribers.

> ❯ Noting it under "upcoming speaking engagements" at the end of your e-zine.

> ❯ Creating an "upcoming speaking engagements" link in the press room of your Website.

> ❯ Notification to your alumni newsletter and associations who print member news in their publications.

> ❯ A signature file on the bottom of all outgoing e-mail messages, including discussion groups (discussed in Chapter 10).

> ❯ In the resource box of articles you publish on the Internet that link back to a page on your Website where your engagement is described in depth.

How to Negotiate Perks in Exchange for a Free Talk

Professionals who are motivated to speak in order to build buzz for their business are often expected to speak for free. However, they can often recoup their expenses by savvy negotiating.

Here are some great benefits aggressive speakers can negotiate:

> ❯ The mailing list of the attendees.

> ❯ An endorsement.

> ❯ Free hotel rooms, meals, and entrance to the conference.

> ❯ Having your company literature sent out free with the conference kits sent to attendees.

> ❯ An audiotape of your presentation. Try to bargain for the rights to reproduce and distribute it.

> ❯ A videotape of your presentation. Try to bargain for the rights to reproduce and distribute it.

> ❯ A percentage of all sales generated by your audiotape or videotape.

> ❯ The association or organization buying your book or product for all attendees, with the proceeds going to you.

In addition to what you can get from the association or organization, try to find a sponsor who will pay you a fee in order to boost their image in the eyes of their target market. Nancy Michaels, author of *Perfecting Your Pitch*, looks for sponsors who are trying to sell to female owners of small businesses. Consider your market and find sponsors accordingly.

Conference vendors can also sponsor and pay your fee, but it's a good idea to consider what you can do for them in return. Kare Anderson, a popular speaker on communication issues, agrees to interview vendor sponsors on one side of an audiotape about their businesses. The other side of the tape features her *Make Yourself Memorable* audio program. The tape is distributed free to conference attendees, giving the vendor sponsors more visibility and pleasing the meeting planners or association who hired her.

How to Develop and Deliver a Dynamic Presentation

Before you create your talk, think of what your audience most wants to know. If you've been speaking on your topic for a while, you can usually predict the information they crave. Even so, the best speakers are people who take the simple yet necessary step of customizing their information for their specific audience.

Research and Surveys: Secret Weapons for Effective Talks and Workshops

Surveying attendees in advance of your preparation alerts you to specific issues they want to see addressed. Even better, you will be able to incorporate survey responses in your talk, thus showing the audience the energy you put into the presentation and providing colorful, real-life anecdotes and situations at the same time.

When addressing a special "Media Savvy Lab" for the National Speakers Association at their national headquarters, I surveyed the attendees (a mix of speaker/authors seeking media attention) well before the conference with the specific objective of finding authors with personal "success stories" of how they received free publicity for their books that I could use in the course of my presentation.

Once these stories were identified, I loaded images of the "success story" books into a PowerPoint presentation and used them as visuals as I verbally described publicity techniques their peers used that worked. The result was enhanced attention, involvement, and retention.

To customize a speech on confident presentation skills to be given to The Boston Security Analysts Society (BSAS), I sent an e-mail with three simple questions:

> ❯ Did they give presentations internally, as in reporting to their boss in a meeting, or did they present to clients?

> ❯ What were some of the real-life issues they faced when giving presentations?

> ❯ What questions did they expect to have answered during my presentation?

The response rate was an unprecedented 98 percent, with virtually all attendees asking the same questions:

1. I know my material, but when I'm called to deliver an opinion during a staff meeting, I freeze—what can I do?

2. How can I jack up confidence before a presentation?

3. How can I keep my audience interested in my presentation?

In the course of giving the presentation, I could see attendees visibly relax as "their" question was answered, and they received reassurance that others in the room shared the same concerns. For the speaker, surveys take the guesswork out of figuring what the audience needs to know and delivering the exact information they crave.

Organizing Your Talk

Once you know the information your audience expects to learn, organization is simple, as it consists of:

❭ An introduction.

❭ A body.

❭ A conclusion and call to action.

Begin With the End in Mind

Begin constructing your talk with the conclusion. *Why?* Your last words are really the only thing your audience will remember from your speech. Too many speakers, nervous about being on the podium, conclude their talk in a rush and run off the platform. Others make the mistake of concluding their talk and then taking questions, which leaves them vulnerable to a hostile or rambling question. Worse, the audience leaves with the voice of the last person to ask the question in their minds, and your call to action is long forgotten.

Try scripting a strong conclusion. When you finish the body of your presentation, briefly sum up the points you have made and tell the audience you will take questions for 10 minutes, and then make your concluding points.

Create an Attention-Getting Introduction

The purpose of the introduction is to stimulate the audience's interest for the talk to come. You must establish the timeliness and relevance of your talk to your audience in your very first sentence. Consider that each member of the audience is thinking, *"What's in it for me?"* You must assure them as soon as possible that they will be rewarded for their careful attention with solid "how to" information.

Asking a question and for a show of hands is a good way of grabbing an audience's attention, as it can provide a quick survey of an audience's concerns and forces an audience to become immediately involved.

You can also begin with a startling statistic or statement to shock an audience into paying attention. People, you may recall, are motivated by the promise of pleasure or the fear of pain, so the more emotional you can make your introduction and tap into your audience's hopes and fears, the more you will personally involve them.

Creating the Body of Your Presentation

The body of your presentation is a single key message divided into three subpoints.

Each of the subpoints is a unit of information that serves to underscore your key message. Furthermore, each of the subpoints must be supported by a mix of facts, anecdotes, and statistics, because people learn in a variety of ways.

Let's say a Realtor is giving a public talk about why his audience must act now and buy a house. He's surveyed his audience, knows their concerns, and can even use some of the concerns to add color as anecdotes in his talk. He is also sure of his call to action, which is to buy real estate now while interest rates are historically low. He has planned his introduction as well, which asks, "How many of you are concerned if homes will continue to increase in value or if you buy now, you'll face a sliding market?"

In the body of his talk, he plans to convince his audience that the time to buy is now, and will support it with three key points:

1. Mortgage rates are historically low.

2. Over a period of 30 years, no one ever lost money on a home.

3. There's no "right time" to jump on the bandwagon.

The first point can be supported by facts and statistics from government sources and an anecdote about the days in the 1980s when people were paying rates of 18 percent, intimating that mortgage rates might again go up that high.

The second point can be supported by more government statistics, along with an anecdote about a person who stretched himself to buy a home at the top of the market in 1974 and has increased his investment 100 percent in 2004.

The third point can also include statistics, but here, near the close and call to action, what would be more effective are several anecdotes about people who got on the housing bandwagon at different times (high interest rates, lower home rates, and vice versa) and still managed to come out ahead.

Calming Anxiety and Enhancing Confidence at the Podium

Projecting confidence during a presentation makes you sound more credible and authoritative. Yet the very thought of speaking in public fills many experts with anxiety.

Public speaking puts us in a situation where our most primal, universal needs are put in jeopardy. Instinctively, we all have a need for approval, security, and to be seen and accepted as an "insider" by the group rather than as an outsider.

When we stand before a seated group of our peers or prospects, we leave the safety and security of being part of the group to being *observed and judged by them*. Perfectionists and others who place key importance on the quality of their work are often among the most anxious.

The first thing to remember is that there is really no such thing as perfection, at least in giving a speech. Instead, focus on the words of Roman Orator Cato the Elder nearly 2,000 years ago: *"Grasp the subject and the words will follow."* Think about the *message* you want to communicate with your audience.

Practice is also essential for calming anxiety and enhancing confidence. A typical characteristic of people who lean toward being perfectionists is that they spend a great deal of time perfecting their message, but fail to practice (in front of friends, family, or a mirror) so that they re-create the talk as they plan to give it.

Create an Emotional Bond With Your Audience

Another way to reduce anxiety is to turn your audience into your friends before presentation begins. Greet attendees as they arrive and introduce yourself around the room to create an emotional bond with your audience.

Likability goes a long way to ensuring a supportive audience.

Nido Qubein, a world-famous speaker and successful entrepreneur, radiates the kind of energy that has enabled several generations of audiences to emotionally bond with him immediately. Defining this quality in absolute terms is impossible. It could be the way he uses simple, easy-to-understand stories to help an audience understand his key points or the reassuring tone of his voice.

As you develop in your speaking career, be certain to record the high points of what worked in your presentation after each talk. You will soon discover that surprisingly simple things you do, such as chatting with the attendees, can win an audience over. Or maybe you win an audience over by unscripted humor you periodically (and unconsciously) inject into your talk. Whatever it is, note it—and practice it.

Employ Vocal Variety to Enhance Your Stories

Most of us automatically vary our pitch, speed, and volume when telling stories to children. Even though the members of your audience are adults, seasoned professional speakers can verify the audience enjoys the "story magic" that enables them to map a concept to myth or an individual's life experience.

Professional actors advise that when they "tell" a story in a play or film, they do not simply speak their lines. Instead, they visualize the event as if they were witnessing it again as they speak. Because there is no a film screen for the audience to view the story as he or she speaks it, an actor will employ vocal variety to emotionally connect to the audience and telepathically convey the scene.

Repeat Phrases to Encourage Retention

During a highly memorable session at the Publishers Marketing Association's annual conference called PMA-U, publicist Raleigh Pinsky studded her talk on Internet publicity by demanding that the audience chant "keyword search" at least a dozen times in the 90-minute session.

The chant was fun, enlivened attendees after a long day, and, most importantly, reinforced the message of how important a keyword search is when it comes to getting publicity for your book or business.

Use Vocal Variation to Underscore Transition Points

Visualize your favorite magazine. It is not a bunch of words, jumbled together on a page. Rather, it is a stylized page consisting of headlines, sub-headlines, neat paragraphs, spacing between articles, and often pictures to illustrate a point.

As a listener, you can probably recall a speaker who virtually "threw" information at you so quickly you did not have time to take it all in. As listeners, words come toward us so fast that it's a challenge to keep focused and map what the speaker is saying about our own objectives and goals.

Varying your intonation and employing vocal variety to signal the end of one topic and the beginning of a new topic are excellent ways to help compartmentalize your message so the audience can take it in as a series of small, digestible bites.

Vocal variety and gestures (see the following section) offer your audience three key benefits:

1. They give the audience an opportunity to catch up with you.

2. They provide orientation to where you are in your presentation.

3. They increase retention.

Effective Physical Gestures

Instead of standing stiffly behind the lectern, hands at their sides, good speakers routinely use natural gestures. For example, if you're talking about how disparate parts of your global association can work together, bring your hands together in a "handshake" position to demonstrate solidarity.

Or to underscore your numerical phrases, raise a single finger when announcing your first point. Continue this for each numbered point you make.

Power of the Pause

One of the most powerful things you can do as you speak is pause. When you pause, you give the audience a few extra moments to catch up with their notes or finish mapping what you just said to their own experience. It also serves as an effective divider, separating one thought or concept from another.

Also, try to train yourself to use a pause instead of saying "um" or "you know" as you are searching for a correct word or trying to focus on what you will say next.

Establish Eye Contact With Your Audience

Eye contact with your audience is essential for creating a deep emotional connection and works at a subliminal level. When you make eye contact with your audience, you are speaking directly to them.

In general, try to speak a half sentence to one person, making eye contact, before going on to another person in a different area of the room. Don't feel you have to look at a row of people in order. Concentrate on the friendly faces, but don't linger. If an attendee does not meet your gaze or appears to be anxious, mentally block them out. They are likely distracted by their own issues, which have nothing to do with you.

How to Turn Free Talks Into Dynamic Profit Centers

Many professionals "speak for free" in order to promote their business. Yet you can make a large profit by developing products, such as books, audio CDs, videos, etc., to sell at the back of the room.

Your first objective is to come across like a professional; for that reason, you may feel that product sales will hurt your image. However, realize that your audience needs the information your products can give them. Beyond that, many times they want to take a piece of you home with them to remember your words and wisdom.

John Fuhrman, speaker/consultant and author of *Reject Me—I Love It!* says that he was apprehensive about selling products during his talks, especially if he had accepted a fee. Then one day, a man carrying a tattered copy of *Reject Me* tearfully approached him and said that before he read the book, he had considered suicide, and that Fuhrman is the reason he is alive today. That's when Fuhrman saw how his products could make a positive difference in the world.

Darren LaCroix, author, speaker, and 2001 Toastmasters' World Champion of Public Speaking, agrees that products are an important resource for your audience: "They are your message in formats your audience can take home and listen to again and again. And they are obviously interested in the subject, they want to learn more."

Quick, Inexpensive Ways to Develop Back-of-the-Room Products

Begin by mastering the surprisingly simple art of re-purposing content that is already sitting in your desk drawers, journals, and brochures into products that you can sell at the back of the room. These products can include books (usually Print-On-Demand), audiotapes, audio CDs, CD-ROMs, e-books, and DVDs that have both PowerPoint and video.

With desktop computer technology today, it is both easy and effortless to create professional looking products that establish your credibility and enhance your image. CDs, audio cassettes, and even books and videos can be produced within a fortnight. You can accomplish most of this all on your own with inexpensive software and supplies, or source this out to professionals in the field.

For my own purposes, I carry an Olympus digital recorder to record my speeches, which I can download into my audio editing software and put on a CD. *The result?* An instant audio recording that can sell briskly for $19.95 or more.

Some speakers, such as networking maven Sasha ZeBryk, prefer to skip the technical aspects of producing an audio CD and simply show up at a studio, where the engineer will add a voice-over introduction, music, and professionally edit the audio product.

Peter Bowerman, author of the award-winning book *The Well-Fed Writer*, recently released a six-cassette CD set that he sells for more than $85.00. The CDs are housed in a professional-looking case with vinyl CD sleeves and includes a workbook to accompany the program.

Marilee Driscoll, an expert on long term care planning, speaks at many conferences and sells her six-cassette CD set for as much as $400. Ditto for the *Chicken Soup for the Soul* book-writing team of Mark Victor Hansen and Jack Canfield. At the popular seminars Hansen and Canfield hold, they offer special conference discounts for impulse "on sight" sales. They often throw in a bonus for ordering "on sight," such as other audio recordings and books.

Psychologically, an audio recording carries a higher price than a book, which we are conditioned to see as a $20 item at most. An impressive CD or cassette set with professional cover art and at least six hours of audio is typically priced around $149. The material in a $20 book and $140 audio recording may be identical, but the recording is perceived as a more expensive item. The raw cost of production is comparable for both, depending how you outsource the work.

Following is a list of the kinds of products you can create.

#1 Audio CDs and Cassettes

With the advent of today's technology and a little practice, you can create a professional-sounding and professional-looking CD or cassette in just a few hours. The supplies you will need are:

> ❯ A raw speech recorded on an electronic medium (i.e. CD, cassette, or digital recorder).

> ❯ Audio editing software (i.e., Adobe Audition) or a freelance audio engineer.

> ❯ Blank CDs and labels (if you use an engineer, he will take care of this).

Begin the process by recording one of your talks in a digital format or speaking into your software system with a boom mike. If you own the copyright, you can also duplicate material from a previously recorded audio CD or cassette.

Audio editing software is easy to use. Most software programs come with a few months of technical support, the ability to upgrade to paid support when that period ends, and helpful chat rooms where other users will often volunteer to walk you through the steps.

#2 Videotapes

You have seen infomercials on television. Many companies can be hired to professionally produce a video in which you walk a consumer through your specialty (i.e., market timing, how to buy and sell real estate, daytrading, or persuasive selling techniques), but you also have more inexpensive options.

Landy Chase, a national speaker specializing in sales, created a video by hiring a friend to run three video cameras and inviting even more friends to fill in as audience members while he gave his presentation. The price? The cost of the camera rentals, video editing, and some pizza. On the other hand, Darren LaCroix, 2001 Toastmasters' World Champion of Public Speaking, simply hired cameramen to tape his speaking appearances, and then had the various tapes professionally edited.

#3 Books

This includes books published by traditional publishers, books you self-publish, and Print-On-Demand books (see Chapter 7).

#4 Electronic Books (e-books)

E-books are most commonly used as downloadable products. If you don't have time to create a physical book, sell electronic books on discs at your events.

#5 Booklets

A booklet is a collection of practical tips an audience can put to immediate use. Create a tip-oriented booklet about the concepts covered in your book.

How to "Sell" From the Platform Without Sounding Like a Salesperson

Once you realize that your audience wants and needs your products to reach their objectives, it will be easier for you to sell. Simply remember that image is everything and you are giving the talk to enhance your professional expertise. Resist the temptation to turn your talk into a commercial.

Recently, a top speaker held an all-day session at an enormous conference hall in Boston, where attendees (or their companies) paid upwards of $300 to attend. Every hour, 15 minutes was spent promoting his books and tapes, and with every passing minute, my trust in this "famous" speaker and consultant waned.

Humorist Darren LaCroix suggests that you give your pitch a hefty dose of fun. Also, he advises professionals to record their own product commercial "live" and perfect it.

Given that your main objective in giving the seminar is enhancing your credibility in addition to getting your name in the news, you don't want to come across as crass and commercial. Yet at the same time, you want to sell more products.

Here are some tips and techniques to help you promote with class:

1. **Hold your book or product up as you speak.**

   This is a very effective technique. When you change topics, pick up your book and say something like, "That's what gave me the idea for Chapter 3, in which I surveyed 100 millionaires to find their secrets of success."

   However, be warned that if someone asks you a question, resist the temptation to say "You'll have to read my book." Remember the adage, "The more you tell, the more you sell."

2. **Give the book or product away early in the seminar.**

   You might want to kick things off with an energetic start by finding a reason to give the book away, and have as many hands see it as they pass it to the lucky winner. Speaker, author, and consultant John Fuhrman likes to chat with attendees before the seminar. If he finds someone has a birthday coming up, he asks them to sit in the back row. When the seminar begins, he announces he will give his book away to an attendee nearing their birthday. Of course, this attendee is already in the back row. Fuhrman asks someone in the front row to pass the book down to the lucky winner, allowing everyone to get a good look at it as it is handed back.

3. **Have an enlarged poster of your product on stage.**

   This sends a clear but subtle reminder you have a product to sell. I expand on the typical book poster by having a 6-foot tall banner emblazoned with my book cover and other symbols that reinforce my credibility, such as the logo for one of my associations.

4. **Have an inviting-looking "sell table."**

   Every trade show veteran knows that colorful candy is a huge draw. Many other speakers swear by having a red cloth that shows off your products nicely.

5. **Use bullets.**

   Create a bulleted list of the benefits your book offers, using language such as "3 Secrets of..." or "5 Ways to...."

6. **Leave order forms on chairs before attendees arrive, with a special "today only" discount.**

   This is a great way for people to see that you have products to sell before you even begin to speak. As your audience settles into their seats, they will scan the order form to see what you have to offer. The more content-rich your talk, the more they will want to take your information home with them.

I use a variation on this technique. Instead of a loose discount order form on boring white paper, I created business cards with a picture of my book on the front, a 30 percent discount offer (good anytime, though they would have to e-mail me to receive the special Website link), and a bulleted list of benefits they would get from the book on the back of the card.

People keep the business cards and e-mail me for the discount, sometimes months after the event. Loose order forms tend to get lost or tossed.

How to Get Contact Information From Your Audience

Let's say you are putting on a free seminar and people do not need to pre-register. They simply walk in.

How do you get their contact information? The best way is to ask your audience to submit their business cards for a drawing where they could win a free product. When you advertise the drawing, be certain to give the "free product" a monetary value, the higher the better. If you create products yourself, even your most expensive product will not have personally cost you very much. Giving away an hour of consulting is an even more impressive incentive.

Load the cards into your database and follow up with a personalized mass e-mail thanking them for attending and inviting them to subscribe to your free e-zine. Include a link to a sample of your e-zine, state your privacy policy, and assure them they can unsubscribe at any time.

You may also wish to ask attendees for their feedback. If the feedback is as good as it should be, ask permission to use it as a testimonial for your presentations.

Speaking: An Active Component of Your Marketing Plan

Incorporating public speaking into your marketing plan is an effective strategy for building buzz for your business. Many professionals of various industries now send announcements of their latest speaking engagements with their picture in an HTML e-mail, serving to position themselves front and center in the minds of potential clients and colleagues. They also make sure their engagements are noted in their association newsletters, and even in their local community paper.

Memories fade fast, so once your presentation is over, continue the momentum by continuing to write articles for the association or organization's publication, inviting attendees to join your mailing list or making a special offer to attendees on your services or products. This can mean the opportunity to buy your product at a lower price for a set period of time or the opportunity for them to take advantage of a free half hour of personal consulting or consultation via e-mail.

Chapter Summary

1. Giving workshops creates awareness among your target market and the media.

2. Find speaking opportunities in your local paper, business journal, and by contacting associations found online or in the *Encyclopedia of Associations*.

3. Write articles for association publications as a way of introducing yourself.

4. Have a template proposal ready to tweak, customize, and send off.

5. If you speak for free, realize you can negotiate perks to make the effort worth your time.

6. Surveys are essential for delivering information your target audience craves.

7. A talk consists of an introduction, body, and conclusion. Your audience will remember the last words of your conclusion, so be sure to craft it well and with a strong call to action.

8. Gestures help your target audience visualize what you are saying.

9. Use a pause in place of "filler words" such as "um" and "you know." A pause also gives an audience time to map your words to their own experience and finish taking notes.

Chapter Assignments

☐ Make your reference librarian your best friend. They can help you easily and quickly find the directories of associations you need for speaking success.

☐ Decide to focus on a few core targets with appeal to your target market. Create a computer file with a template that you will customize to suit the needs of specific audiences. Have the file loaded with testimonials, your picture, and the other material you will need to send to a meeting planner or conference organizer on a moment's notice.

☐ Consider what information you have in your computer files or desk drawers that can form the basis of products you can sell at the back of the room.

☐ If you are apprehensive about public speaking, join a Toastmasters association in your city.

☐ Be certain to spend time on the actual rehearsal of your talk to be more comfortable on the platform.

9

Creating Buzz for Your Business Through Articles

Those who write clearly have readers. Those who write obscurely have commentators.

—Albert Camus, Playwright and Novelist (1913–1960)

Articles are an excellent way to reach and impress your target market with your knowledge and expertise. Each article that is published acts as your own personal foot soldier, spreading your name, message, and area of expertise throughout the universe.

Like authoring a book, your bylined name on an article gives you instant credibility and enhanced prestige. Yet, articles are written in a matter of hours instead of years. Prospects and clients too busy to read an entire book will also appreciate a succinct article focusing on their area of interest.

Why are articles so powerful?

is the leading expert in his field. The publication gives that author/expert the kind of official third-party credibility money just can't buy.

Articles Have Staying Power

Television is fun and glamorous. Yet after the show, your appearance is reduced to a line in your media kit. Unless your personal network and your prospects *watched* the show, they missed the brilliance of your thoughts.

Your articles can be made available to anyone who wants to read them at a moment's notice. You can carry them in your briefcase to distribute during meetings, enclose them with letters you send to clients and colleagues during normal business correspondence, and post them to you Website, where they can be immediately downloaded.

You can also use articles as the basis for a direct mail campaign to send to clients and colleagues in order to solicit referrals, generate leads, and create greater awareness of your services.

Articles Pre-Sell You to Prospects

When prospects come to know your value through your articles, you don't have to be concerned with selling yourself during the initial meeting. Instead, you can focus on better understanding their needs.

Using Articles to Build Your Business

Ken Lizotte, president of the New England chapter of the Institute of Management Consultants and Chief Imaginative Officer of Emerson Consulting Group, Inc., frequently writes articles about consulting and other topics for key publications read by his target audience. To maximize publicity, he gets reprint rights and sends the published articles to clients and prospects, as well as distributes them at association meetings.

This enhances his credibility and prestige with his network, as well as with people who have not yet met him. More importantly, the fact that he is so frequently published by prestigious business publications underscores his ability to get good results for clients who hire him for his article ghostwriting services.

Articles Work 24/7 to Position You as the Expert of Choice

Marketing experts agree that it takes at least seven points of contact (each time your name is seen, heard, or mentioned) for your target audience to recognize your name.

Your article can work for you 24 hours a day, seven days a week, to position you as the expert of choice along with these added advantages:

> ❭ When your name appears in prestigious publications, you can justify raising your fees.

> ❭ When existing clients see your article, they feel reassured they made the right choice and will help you spread the word about your services.

> ❭ When prospects read your approach to your business in a prestigious publication, they are pre-sold before they meet you.

> ❭ Publicity begets more publicity. When journalists read your articles, many will put you in their database as an expert source and you may land interviews with even bigger publications.

> Articles give you valuable content to post on your Website, where prospects can go to learn more about your business.

> You can distribute articles at professional associations and other meetings to stimulate referrals.

> You can turn articles into a series of columns in a publication read each month by your target audience, complete with a picture and resource box giving your contact information.

> You can turn articles into a downloadable e-book or audio CD you can give prospects and customers.

> You can re-purpose a series of articles as the basis of a public talk or seminar.

> You can turn a series of articles into an Internet course for an additional stream of revenue.

> You can use "news" of your article's publication to get your name in newsletters, e-zines, or Websites of local or national branches of associations to which you belong. (For example, members of the Society of Professional Consultants are invited to send news of articles and talks to the monthly print newsletter.)

> You can submit your article to be posted in its entirety on your association's print newsletter or Website. For example, the Institute of Management Consultants Website posts member articles, including their resource boxes.

Articles Attract Positive Outcomes

Jen Singer, author of *14 Hours 'Til Bedtime: A Stay-at-Home Mom's Life in 27 Funny Little Stories*, is also a freelance journalist who authors articles for the big glossy publications read by her target market (*Parenting*, *Family Circle*, *American Baby*, etc.).

Singer advises that experts write for all publications read by their niche markets, big and small alike, because you never know who will read the article and where it can lead. She tells the story of an author who had read her quote in a free regional parenting magazine and ended up interviewing her for a book and an article for the *New York Times*.

"Also," adds Singer, "the head of special events at Lord & Taylor invited me to do book signings this fall at their stores, where they'll buy and give out 150 of my books at each event, after reading an interview I gave in an online newsletter."

The Writing Process: Getting Started

Editors, especially from trade and business publications, are eager for good, solid information to offer their readers. Paul Montelongo, president of his own construction firm and national speaker and sales trainer, successfully writes for hundreds of construction and business trade magazines.

"This way," he says, "I get lots and lots of eyeballs looking at my resource box (see Chapter 10) and going to my Website to find more information. People often buy my products, hire me as a speaker, or engage me as a consultant."

Montelongo's technique involves using the library media directories to research his market and find a publication looking for an article in his area of expertise, sketching out a story with a slant suitable to the publication, and then calling the editor and pitching the story.

Finding Story Ideas

Now that you realize the benefits of writing articles, *how do you start?* Refresh yourself with the concepts in Chapter 1, dealing with how to find story ideas and pitch them to reporters. The process is similar, with editors wanting the same timely, relevant story ideas to service their readers.

One of the most popular ways to frame your information is in the body of a how-to article that gives readers valuable information.

Finding Appropriate Publications and Contact Information

In Chapter 1, you learned to use media directories in the public library to find information on how to reach people in the media. You can use these same directories to find editors, learn their preferred ways of being contacted, and send them your pitch.

Freelance writers make use of *Ulrich's International Periodicals Directory,* a comprehensive guide to the periodical market, listing more than a quarter-million consumer and trade magazines, as well as academic and scholarly publications. Many libraries allow you to use your library card from your home or office to access this electronic resource over the Internet. Also, you might wish to purchase a relatively inexpensive but very convenient resource called *Writer's Market,* which is also available online.

Familiarize Yourself With the Publication You Want to Pitch

Any editor will tell you that the biggest mistake people make is pitching ideas or submitting entire stories to markets they are not familiar with. Before pitching an editor, be clear on the following:

> ❯ Your purpose in writing your article.

> ❯ The target audience you want to reach.

> ❯ What this target market reads.

> ❯ The articles editors usually publish.

Study the Editorial Calendar

Virtually every newspaper and business journal has an editorial calendar in which they list specific themes or a monthly focus. Finding editorial calendars is effortless. Simply type the name of the publication and the words "editorial calendar" in a search engine such as Google.

By studying editorial calendars, you will get a sense of what subjects publications are targeting in the future. Typically, the articles are written by on-staff reporters, but if you have expertise on a topic, you can talk to one of the managing editors to see if you can submit an article of your own.

Accomplish this by calling the publication, explain the specific section of the editorial calendar you want to write for, and find which editor handles that section.

Queries to Editors

A "query" is your story pitch in written form. It must be short and snappy, and command instant attention. Like a book proposal that sometimes seems as if it takes more time and energy to write than the book itself, your query should be carefully shaped so it is short, descriptive, and compelling, yet address and answer any concerns the editor may have.

Once you perfect your query, you will want to pitch it in the right way. Here are some tips:

> Headlines are important. Make sure your headline is catchy and memorable.

> Your query is your sales letter. Sell the editor on the fact your story will inform their readers with relevant, timely information.

> Use facts and statistics to give credibility to your idea.

> Underscore the credentials that qualify you to write on this topic.

> Get the editor's attention with a first sentence that grabs their immediate interest. This often turns out to be the first line of your finished piece.

Perfect your query and send it to the editor in the way they prefer according to the media directories. If you fax or e-mail, feel confident calling to follow up within a week. Have a phone script prepared in the likely event the editor can't remember your pitch.

As you may recall, don't just call to verify they received the information; offer "new news." For example, you might jog their memory by saying, "Hello, this is John Doe. I sent you a query on new trends in financial engineering last week. This article is even more relevant today because of breaking news that suggests XYZ."

Editors Speak Out

I contacted a few editors to share their views on how they like to be pitched.

Amy Schurr, senior managing editor of *Network World*, prefers e-mail pitches, explaining that "along with being able to choose a time to review the pitch when I have time, it's nice to have everything in writing so I can check to see if we've covered that angle before and conduct preliminary research. E-mail also makes it easy to share the idea with another editor here to get his or her input."

Rick Nelson, chief editor of *Test & Measurement World*, offers the following candid advice about pitching your article.

Tips on How to Pitch

1. In e-mail, the subject line should be crystal clear: "Ajax Cleans Super Bowl," not "Press release from my client attached."

2. Put your message in the main body of the e-mail message text. Don't make editors open attachments. Attachments often are corrupted during the e-mail transfer. No editor is going to bother asking you to retransmit (unless you have a previous relationship with that editor). Furthermore, attachments might be blocked by virus programs. And the extra seconds it might take an editor to open an attachment might just be the final straw that pushes him to hit the delete button instead. Go ahead and attach a beautifully formatted Word or PDF document, but make sure the editor can read the plain text to get your message without having to open any attachments. It's the message, not the layout and formatting, that will get an editor's attention.

3. Don't attach a huge high-resolution image file, but do provide a link to where I can download a high-resolution image file from your Website. Editors put everything off until the last minute and might just need some distinctive image to fill a news hole. I may not care too much about Ajax cleaning the Super Bowl, but if a striking image of bubbles filling a stadium could fill a pressing requirement for artwork, and you've told me where I can go to immediately download it, I'll probably run your story.

4. If you are pitching a particular story rather than mass mailing a press release, make the message personal. Do some research. Visit the publication's Website. Don't write: "I'd like to write an article about the service I provide cleaning football stadiums." Do write: "Dear Rick, I see that your magazine carried an article last month on how Ajax is cleaning football stadiums. My company has a new and unique process that cleans Super Bowls in half the time at half the cost. We would be happy to write an article for you about Comet's services. I can also make myself available for an interview."

5. Phone calls are really annoying. They take up a lot of time and are usually not productive. It can take 10 or 15 minutes for a caller and me to determine that her client and my magazine aren't a good fit. That said, calls can be effective if they are properly targeted. This day and age, few people at any level have secretaries that can screen calls, so, more than ever, a persistent caller is likely to reach her target sooner or later. I advise people not to abuse this. As in #4 above, do some research. When you make that call, make sure you have something to offer that

the editor can use. Don't train editors to hang up on you.

6. E-mail is best for now, but e-mail is nearly dead. I get maybe 300 e-mail messages per day that deserve some serious response. That's 300 after I've deleted the amateur-web-cam and herbal-Viagra messages. That's just too much to handle, despite my best intentions. So the ones I do respond to are ones from people or organizations I know, or ones that adhere scrupulously to items 1 through 4 above.

7. Finally, nothing succeeds like face-to-face meetings. The most effective phone call or e-mail message is, "I'll be in Boston next week; may I stop by your office and describe our new Super Bowl cleaning services?" Or, "If you visit our city in the near future, we would be happy to have you interview our executive team and tour our facility."

8. Trade shows are a good way to have a lot of face-to-face meetings in a short period of time. Arrange in advance for a specific time during which editors can visit your booth or hospitality suite. Don't count on an editor just stopping by at some point.

© Rick Nelson

Letters to the Editor and Opinion Pieces

Imagine what it must feel like to arrive at work one morning and find dozens of congratulatory e-mails and voice messages awaiting your arrival. This is what happened to me after the *New York Times* published my letter to the editor.

Write a letter to the editor whenever you read an article you feel merits your comments and you have the authority and credentials to back your claim. When you write a letter to the editor (very easy these days, as the *Wall Street Journal*, *New York Times*, and other top publications have an electronic link on their Website), passion and emotion are very important. You are either outraged by an article and thus feel the need to tell the editor and world about it, or you feel that a reporter perfectly sums up something that has long been on your mind.

It's important to type your full contact information after your letter, as editors like to run your city and state. All in all, writing a letter to the editor is a good way to keep your name in the news by *reacting* to the news instead of shaping it.

Somewhat similar to the letter to the editor is an opinion-editorial, sometimes called an "op-ed." This is a first-person work around 400 to 600 words long that expresses your personal opinions on a specific topic. Newspapers, both local and national, are always eager for timely op-eds that reflect a particular trend, are written by an expert in that particular field, and have impact for the majority of their readers.

There is no set formula for writing an opinion piece, but editors agree that you should make your strongest point up front, and then spend the rest of the op-ed making your case with facts and/or a strong emotional anecdote and then concluding with a strong call to action. To ensure you are on target, make it a habit to study the op-eds of the publication you are trying to pitch for a few weeks.

Building Buzz Through Syndication

Syndicating your articles is a dynamic way to build buzz for your business. Though authors make very little money from syndication, the real reward is having your target market read your words of wisdom on a regular basis. Adding the words "syndicated columnist" to your resume also gives you an additional patina of glamour.

Robert Otto, senior product marketing manager at DYMEC, Inc., has received the following benefits from his syndicated column:

> ❯ Recognition as an expert in the community.

> ❯ People seeking him out for expert advice.

> ❯ Being approached by various groups and organizations to give talks to their group.

> ❯ Personal gratification when people recognize him from having read his column.

In addition, Otto claims his column contributed to his securing a senior product marketing role where he reports directly to the CEO of his company. The easiest way to get syndicated is to have a syndicating service seek you out and pitch you to newspaper editors with enormous pomp and circumstance. The largest syndicates include United Features Syndicate and Universal Press Syndicate. Visit their Websites on the Internet in order to download submission guidelines.

Because syndication is a competitive field, the realistic way to become a syndicated author is to do it yourself. This means contacting editors and showing them samples of your work.

Your first step is to create a series of six to 12 columns on a specific topic related to your area of expertise. Make sure your writing is lively and offers valuable content. Think of a catchy name for your column, and remember that the title of each article must grab immediate attention.

Next, if you have a Website, create a folder and load the articles onto your site in HTML. Be certain the site is fast-loading (avoid high-resolution pictures that will slow it down), but do try to make it as attractive as possible. Find examples to emulate by searching Google using words like "syndicated author."

Finally, consult media directories to create a database of newspaper editors, making sure the section they cover is appropriate to the theme of your column. At this point, you will create a short, snappy e-mail query that introduces your column, as well as underscores its benefits to readers and your qualifications for writing it in three to four tightly focused sentences. Provide a link to the Web page you have created so that interested editors can click to your Website and view your biography and scan your columns at their leisure.

Syndication is a numbers game, so the more editors you contact, the more success you will have. As you only need two publications to carry your column to be called a syndicated columnist, success can very soon be yours.

Pricing remains a difficult issue, with many authors syndicating for free and others receiving literal pennies for their work. As your objective is to get your name and expertise out into the world, realize that your monetary reward will come in the form of new clients and purchasers of your products. Virtually all newspapers allow columnists to include a brief resource box listing their e-mail address and Website.

Turning Articles Into Books

Many professionals want to sit down and write a book but simply don't have the time. One way to get around this is to break the writing project down into manageable parts. Begin by creating a table of contents consisting of 10 chapters, and break each chapter into five to 10 key points or issues to be discussed. Then, systematically turn each of those five to 10 key points in each chapter into an article. Take each group of articles and weave them seamlessly into a chapter. When you have your 10 chapters, you have a book.

Chris Vasiliadis, owner of self-promotion firm Signature Faces, Inc., took a bottoms-up approach in building her book: "I began by brainstorming a list of article topics consistent with my company's mission, plus addressing common questions I'm asked by clients and related scenarios I frequently encounter. After that, I sorted the topics into logical chunks in a flow that makes sense. For the sorting process, I used index cards: I wrote one topic on each card, then grouped related themes together in different mini-stacks, and finally arranged the cards in a single deck, in logical order. Now I'm writing and publishing individual articles one at a time, as these articles will ultimately generate the book's chapters. I'll fill in the informational and table of content gaps as necessary to complete the book in a usable, practical format. As I publish each article, I'm creating buzz and obtaining reader feedback that I'll ultimately incorporate into the final book content."

Chapter Summary

1. Articles are an effective way to promote your expertise and build your business.

2. You can use articles as the basis of a future book.

3. Use news of your article's publication to get your name in association newsletters.

4. Place articles in publications where they will be seen by your target audience.

5. In addition to articles, writing opinion pieces and letters to the editor can get you additional publicity.

6. Responding to a subject listed in a publication's editorial calendar is a good way to understand what kind of article and information the editor needs.

7. To get your article idea accepted by an editor, you must be as familiar as possible with the publication.

8. As you create your pitch or query, pay special attention to the title of your article. Take care to make it as vibrant and snappy as possible.

9. Editors give queries a two-second glance before moving on to the next query. Learn to grab their attention by your use of strong, vivid language and meeting the needs of their target audience.

10. Investigate the media directories available at your local library to find contact information for editors, and also inquire about how to use the libraries electronic resources from your own home.

11. Consider self-syndication to leverage the energy spent on a single article.

Chapter Assignments

☐ Brainstorm a list of publications your target audience reads on a regular basis. Ask yourself if someone influences the buying decisions of this market, and if this "influencer" (such as a human resources executive) might read different publications.

☐ Create an article writing schedule. Resolving to research, query, and write one article a month is a realistic goal.

☐ If you plan to write a book someday, give careful consideration to who it would appeal to and what it would be about. Resolve to write articles that could be incorporated into your book. You might also consider writing your table of contents, breaking each chapter up into eight to 10 sections, and turning each section into an article.

☐ If you already have a book, turn excerpts from it into articles of varying lengths.

☐ Study the example of a personalized mass e-mail to editors pitching three to four prewritten stories, and decide if this would work for you, considering your media objectives.

☐ Consider self-syndication as a means of getting additional exposure. What would be your topic? What newspapers, ideally, would carry your column? Brainstorm six to 12 topics you can easily write.

10

Building Buzz, Brand, and Business Through Online Promotion

Look before, or you'll find yourself behind.
—Benjamin Franklin, Writer, Inventor, and Philosopher (1706–1790)

When it comes to building buzz for your "brick and mortar" *or* online business, you will find that building a keyword- and content-rich Website is one of the most efficient ways to position yourself as the expert in your field and attract media attention.

Perhaps you've felt a sting of jealousy when a *Wall Street Journal* reporter quoted a half-dozen of your competitors for a story, but somehow never got around to calling you.

How did I miss out?, you might wonder.

The answer might be as simple as the keywords on your Website.

Reporters find experts in a variety of ways, but the most common method is through the Internet. Rushed and on deadline, reporters type keywords that relate to their story into their favorite search engines. For example, if a reporter is looking for an expert on food safety he'd enter the words "food safety" plus the word "expert" into a search engine.

When the results pop up on the screen, he quickly scrolls through the experts' sites, looking for what is called a "media room" or "press room" as a link on their top navigation bar.

The media room holds all the information a reporter needs to qualify you as an expert, so if you don't have one, you better create one *fast!*

Elements of a Media Room

1. **Biography** (include short and long versions).

   Keep this updated! Journalists will often cut and paste your information and insert it in their articles. This is especially true if they can't reach you before publication.

2. **Picture of yourself in various resolutions.**

   Often, a newspaper will want to run a picture of you. The low resolution of a typical Web image will blur on the page, so they will need to download a 300 dpi image.

3. **Prestigious associations and distinctions.**

   Associations mark you as a more credible source. Be certain to explain association distinctions, such as the CMC (Certified Management Consultant) from the Institute of Management Consultants or the CSP (Certified Speaking Professional) from the National

Speakers Association, or the many others awarded by high-profile associations.

4. **Interviews.**

Journalists like to see how you stand on specific issues and what makes you different from your competition. Interview yourself using questions you think a journalist would ask you, and post the questions and answers using a *Q & A* format on your Website. Having interview questions on your site will be a lifesaver if a radio host loses the questions you sent him in advance and needs to have questions to ask you on the air.

5. **A library of articles you have written or have been written about you.**

Articles, both as links to other sites and in full text, are great credibility boosters. They reinforce your status as the leading expert in your field.

6. **A list of press releases.**

If you don't have press releases on your site, get busy. Create them on a weekly or monthly basis, piggybacking on an issue hot in the news. Be certain they are filled with keywords the media would use when looking for an expert of your ilk. Also, post them on free posting sites like PR Web (*www.prweb.com*).

7. **A list of past radio and TV interviews.**

The secret of making media appearances pay off for you seven days a week, 24 hours a day, instead of the actual four to six minutes you are on the air, is to leverage the media appearance on your Website, in print, in introductions to your speeches, and so forth. Create a running list of all media appearances and keep it updated.

8. A running list of future story ideas.

Journalists are not mind readers. Help them understand the variety of ways they can tap into your expertise by providing story ideas. Keep this list of story ideas timely with new developments in the news.

9. A video clip of yourself being interviewed on a TV show.

A prestigious television clip marks you as an immediate expert.

10. An audio clip of yourself being interviewed on the radio.

Audio clips from radio appearances are good, but keep them short. Be certain to ask the station in advance to record your interview.

11. Prestigious endorsements of your book.

If you have written a book and well-known people have endorsed it, it belongs in your media room.

12. An up-to-date list of future speaking engagements.

If you speak, put your future engagements on your media room page. Keep it updated. You can also add endorsements from the people who engaged you to speak.

Why include a running list of story ideas?

Isn't the journalist already working on a story?, you may wonder.

Why should I feed him more?

The answer is that freelance journalists like to "multipurpose" their stories. If they are writing on one topic and see a list of related story ideas on your site, they may use your stories and quote you as an expert to quickly spin off a number of other stories for other publications.

Spinning sources and core stories into a variety of angles is how freelance journalists make additional income.

On my Website (*www.BuildingBuzz.com*), this is what my list of running story ideas looks like. Know that you may also add a list of topics you can speak on (see list below story ideas):

Story Ideas

After hearing about your readership and specific story angle, Marisa D'Vari will provide exclusive information, quotes, and additional experts for you on these evergreen story topics:

Marketing and Publicity

▸ How entrepreneurs can position themselves above the competition.

▸ How to shape and define your brand through logo and slogan.

▸ How to use the media to enhance your image.

▸ How to repurpose speeches and articles into cash and credibility.

Networking and Business Etiquette

▸ Classic networking mistakes and how to fix them.

▸ How to remember names at social events.

▸ How to handle a business lunch interview.

▸ How to take clients to dinner.

Public Speaking

▶ How non-speakers can quickly put together an effective speech.

▶ How to conquer anxiety before a speech.

▶ How to telegraph confidence.

Book Publishing

▶ How to repurpose speeches and articles into cash and credibility.

▶ How to choose between traditional and self publishing.

▶ How to effectively outline and write a book.

▶ How to market and publicize a book.

▶ How to use your Website to attract clients.

▶ How to use an e-zine as a free marketing tool.

▶ How to build an online seminar.

D'Vari may also be able to provide relevant insight for any articles that cover some aspect of the following subjects:

▶ Subconscious behavior.

▶ Body language.

▶ Credibility.

Make It Easy for Reporters to Contact You

Reporters are notorious for being on deadline, and they need an expert *now*. Provide them with all available methods of contact, including a cell phone if you feel comfortable with being on call 24/7.

Establishing "Top of Mind" Awareness for Your Website

Turn your Website into a voracious marketing tool that works for you seven days a week, 24 hours a day to attract new clients and customers and bring in additional streams of revenue.

Your Website is the nucleus of your online promotion. It must have three key elements to draw the traffic you desire:

1. A memorable domain name that is easy to spell.

2. Free information and rich content in the form of articles and hard-to-find links.

3. Keywords in HTML that are frequently used in the text of individual pages.

One of the first considerations in building buzz on the Web is to determine a domain name that is easy to remember and spell, yet also reinforces the theme of your business. Even if you already have named your site, consider buying one that reflects these principles.

You will use your domain name to brand your business in dozens, even hundreds, of ways. First, you will put your domain name on your stationery and collateral material. Second, you will realize the value of discarding your AOL, MSN, EarthLink, or other generic Internet provider e-mail address in favor of adopting your domain name as the end of your e-mail address.

For example, even though my domain's Internet provider is EarthLink, my e-mail address is not mdvari@earthlink.net. I've used the tools available to EarthLink customers to "forward" mail addressed to my EarthLink account to my *www.BuildingBuzz.com* domain, so that people e-mail me at mdvari@BuildingBuzz.com.

Not only does this build brand recognition with each e-mail I send, but it also puts the "curiosity factor" into play as people want to see what kind of helpful information a site with this name would offer.

Use Your Domain Extension When Speaking of Your Company Name

Tami DePalma and Kim Dushinski, owners of the PR firm MarketAbility, simply used that name until the late 1990s when speaking of their business. Then they got savvy and began to speak of their company as MarketAbility.com, so that folks hearing them at conferences or other talks would know how they could be found on the Web.

When you speak of your company and include the ".com" extension, you are helping listeners help themselves by finding you on the Internet.

Using Your Website to Attract Clients and Establish Credibility

In today's world, everyone rushes to the Internet to get the scoop on you and your business. Set your Website up properly, and you will establish immediate credibility with journalists and prospects.

Just as a professional wardrobe helps you establish credibility, the look and usability of your Website will reassure people you are safe to do business with. Following are the do's and don'ts of a professional-looking site.

6 Elements of an Effective Website

1. **A good navigation bar.**

   The navigation bar at the top or side of your Website should be clear and identical on all pages. Do not forget a link called "Home," because most people who find you through a search engine would land on a page other than "Home."

2. **Avoid long-winded Flash introductions.**

   Yes, Flash technology looks cool—but few people have the patience to watch it on their computers and will move on to the next site. The same holds true for pictures that flash or make noise.

3. **Give your unique value proposition as quickly as possible.**

   The top portion of your Website is valuable real estate. Let people know what they can expect to find on the site as quickly as possible, and preferably on every page. For example, the banner of my site says "Attract Clients and Establish Yourself as the Expert of Choice With Free Media Publicity."

4. **Keep sentences short and concise.**

   People skim on the Web. Tell them what you can do for them in as few words as possible.

5. **Replace the words "I" and "We" with the word "You."**

   The Web is a place where people short on time go to get fast, free information. When you use the word "you," you immediately show the prospect what you can do for them.

6. Spelling errors and dead links can be fatal.
Your Website must look as if it is frequently updated, fresh, and professional. Anything less will have folks running to your competition.

———————————

Now that your Website looks professional, you can fill it with content so visitors can access data, including frequently asked questions, tip sheets, and backgrounders about your business. You can even make it possible for people to buy downloadable products that they can pay for and receive without any effort on your part.

Today your Website can be used as:

1. A brochure where Web surfers can go to learn more about your company.

2. A place where prospects can verify your credibility.

3. A marketing vehicle to collect the e-mail and/or physical addresses of prospects.

4. A venue where interested customers can purchase your products, both physical and downloadable.

Let's look at each key point in detail.

Websites as Brochures

In the past, entrepreneurs, professionals, and corporations created four-color brochures in order to let prospects know about the services they offer. Besides being expense to create, these paper brochures are easily outdated.

Today, the trend is increasingly in favor of using one's Website on the Internet to replace the old-fashioned, paper brochure. Benefits include the:

> ❭ Ability to update and change key information on a daily basis.

> ❭ Ability to change prices and offer specials at a moment's notice.

> ❭ Ability to change wording or description of products/services quickly.

> ❭ Ability to measure results of various promotional campaigns.

Websites as Credibility

Establish your credibility by listing the following on your Website:

> ❭ A partial client list.

> ❭ Testimonials from satisfied clients.

> ❭ Your educational background and professional accolades.

> ❭ Upcoming speaking engagements.

> ❭ Information on how long you have been in business.

Websites as Marketing Tools

Direct marketing through the post office requires expensive graphic design, clever copywriting, and postage. Permission-based marketing via e-mail is inexpensive and effective in numbers.

Capture e-mail addresses by offering a monthly e-zine and motivate people to join by allowing them to click on a sample, assuring them of your privacy policy, and offering a free gift, such as a downloadable special report when they subscribe.

Websites as Online Stores

Increasingly, the Web is being used as a place to sell content, rather than give key information free. You can package and sell your intellectual property in a number of ways, both physical and downloadable.

How to Sell Products and Services From Your Website

Selling products on your Website creates additional streams of income in addition to acting as marketing tools on their own. If you have given speeches and written articles or a book, you have a treasure trove of intellectual capital sitting around in your file cabinets.

Marilee Driscoll, who established herself as an expert in the area of long term care planning, is now selling products based on how other experts can use her techniques to get free publicity. Jane Pollak, a national speaker who established a niche reviving and teaching the artisan tradition of decorative eggs, received national television exposure for her work and went on to create "how to" publicity products, as well as her book *Soul Proprietor: 100 Lessons from a Lifestyle Entrepreneur*.

Marcia Yudkin, a marketing guru and author of more than 11 books, has parlayed her expertise into e-books, audio courses, home study courses, and special reports in addition to a lucrative speaking/consulting career. Darren LaCroix, Toastmasters' 2001 World Champion of Public Speaking, parlayed his success into a series of audiotape and videotape products.

The secret of successful product creation is to:

❭ Find the problems of your target audience and provide specific solutions.

❭ Provide those solutions in a variety of formats, including:

▸ Books.

▸ Downloadable e-books.

▸ Audio CDs.

▸ Streaming audio.

▸ Printed manuals or special reports.

▸ Downloadable manuals or special reports.

▸ Printed tip-oriented booklets.

▸ Downloadable tip-oriented booklets.

▸ E-mail consulting.

▸ Phone consulting.

▸ Telephone seminars.

▸ Webinars (Web and voice-based seminars in real time).

▸ Online courses.

Slicing and Dicing for Profits

The key to adding value to subscribers, clients, and prospects while making additional streams of income for yourself is to:

1. Create an assortment of specific niche products.

2. Create each specific niche product in a variety of formats.

Let's assume you have written a book and own the rights to that book. Realizing that not everyone has the time to read a 200-page book and most people are searching for instant information, you can take chunks of content from the book and create individual products, such as e-books or tip-oriented booklets for immediate download.

If you don't have a book but write articles, consider turning the different topics of your articles into bulleted lists or online tip-oriented booklets.

If you give talks and presentations, consider selling the audio or video recordings of your talks. Software such as Adobe Audition can help you create a professional-sounding product on your personal computer. You can also transcribe your talk or presentation and sell it as a downloadable PDF product.

If you don't write or speak publicly, consider the questions clients always seem to be asking you. If you give seminars, what do audiences ask you? Repackage that material in the form of a PDF file or an audio file. Also, recognize that many people on the Internet today have also had success interviewing other experts in a telephone seminar, and then, with the other person's permission, selling the resulting interview as an audio product.

Immediate Downloads for Faster Sales

In a seminar given to the Publishers Marketing Association, self-publishing guru Dan Poynter, a pioneer in the field of downloadable articles, gave his audience food for thought when he explained that *CliffsNotes* (the familiar yellow and black study guides that save students time reading classic books) are priced higher for electronic Internet downloads than the physical product. *Why?* People are cramming for an exam and need the information *immediately*.

People use keywords on the Internet to find free information in order to solve a particular problem and to get immediate gratification. Savvy entrepreneurs are creating Web pages full of information with specific, relevant keywords to attract people to their site. The pages give some compelling free information, yet end with a link to buy a downloadable product.

Finding a Secure Online Retailer

To find a secure retailer, perform an Internet search, ask fellow members of your favorite Internet discussion groups, or feel free to check out the secure online retailers I use, which are *www.ccnow.com* for shipping physical products and *www.clickbank.com* for downloadable products.

Driving Traffic to Your Site

Driving traffic to your site is an ongoing process. It involves keeping information on your site fresh and current, keeping an eye on developments in search engine optimization, and creating interest in your site through the following:

> ❯ Online article distribution and syndication (with a direct link to your Website).

> ❯ Print article distribution and syndication (covered in Chapter 9) with a printed link to your Website.

> ❯ Creating a compelling "signature line" that motivates recipients of any e-mail you send to click on your site for more information or a free gift.

> Posting helpful information via e-mail to Internet discussion group sites to establish yourself as an expert in your field and a "personality," making sure to include your signature line.

Keywords: The Heart of Your Web Marketing Campaign

Did you ever wonder why some sites come up first on the results of a search engine, and other sites appear on page 10? The field of Internet search engine optimization is always changing as search engines such as Google apply new algorithms to search technology. Yet filling your Website with the appropriate keywords remains a consistently effective way to attract a stream of highly directed traffic from your target audience.

As you probably know, keywords are words or short phrases you or your Webmaster place in the keyword meta tag area of your site.

These keywords are used in your text copy and in the code behind the page. For example, keywords I use on my site include words and phrases like "PR," "public relations," "promotions," "publicity," "how to write a press release," "sample of a press release," "media release," "news release," and more. Although a press release, media release, and news release are basically the same document, people use all of these terms when choosing keywords to search, so I made sure that all these terms were included.

The objective for the next step is to create a long list of keywords your target audience may use to find you and your business.

You will want to think *outside the box* so you can get the kind of unique keywords and short descriptive phrases specific enough to set you apart from competitors in your field. Sometimes, depending on the service you offer, this can be as simple as adding your city to the list of keywords.

To find the variety of names people may use when searching for an expert in your field, ask friends and family for contributions. Sneak around the Web by visiting your top-ranked competitors and view the keywords they use to describe their businesses. Do this on Internet Explorer through the View menu by selecting "Source." Now, look through the HTML coding until you see the following:

<meta name="keywords" content="..."

Do you see the two quotation marks after the word "content"? This is where your keywords and key phrases go, separated by commas.

The objective here is not to "steal" keywords, but to see how others are using them and sprinkling them through their text.

You can also find keywords at *www.wordtracker.com*, which offers a free trial of their fee-based service. During the free trial period, you can drill down and select specific phrases potential buyers and journalists would use to find your business.

Finally, if you have a Website tracking service (this is free with many Internet service providers), check your logs and find the top 10 or 20 keywords that brought people to your site.

Once you have your long list of keywords, determine which words and phrases best describe your business, and which words would most likely be used by people trying to find information, a service, or product in your field.

The magic of using keywords with search engine optimization, at least at the time of this writing, is not just stuffing the keywords within the meta tags; it's the larger issue of deciding what keywords to use on what specific pages, and ensuring that the actual text of each specific page matches all the keywords you use in the meta tags. The more you use keywords in your text copy, the more relevant you are to search engines. The trick is to use and repeat keywords without compromising the readability of your text copy. It's a balance between writing for the search engines and writing for your reader.

Search engines scan for keywords that match as closely as possible the text on the Web page. The more you repeat keywords, and the higher they appear on your text page, the higher your ranking and the easier journalists, clients, and customers will find you.

Create, Distribute, and Syndicate Online Articles

Getting your articles in print publications is great for your credibility. But even though there may be a resource box at the end of your article, by the time someone reading it gets to the computer, they may have forgotten your name, Web address, and your special offer.

This is one of the many reasons why it's a good idea to write and distribute online articles on a regular basis. Others include:

> When people read your online article, they can immediately click on your Website to take advantage of your special offer or click for more information.

> When potential clients or customers perform a search on your name, all your articles come up, increasing your credibility.

> ❭ You can submit the same article to many different Websites, thus getting more return for time spent writing the article.

The best articles give practical "how-to" advice about how to solve a problem facing your target audience. Also, remember that when you write articles for an online audience, it's important to:

> ❭ Create a list of keywords your target audience would use if they wanted to find articles or get information on the problem your product or service solves. You want to use those keywords in the headline and body (especially the first paragraph) of your text.

> ❭ Get to the point as quickly as possible, preferably in your opening sentence.

> ❭ Succinctly outline the steps or a course of action that will help a reader solve a problem.

> ❭ Keep the article to 500 words or less.

> ❭ Keep sentences and paragraphs short.

> ❭ End with a firm call to action.

> ❭ Use a time-sensitive offer and strong benefits in your resource box to motivate the reader to click on your site immediately.

In addition to keywords, your article's title should combine elements of surprise and curiosity, as well as contain a strong emotional hook. Effectively, your article title must stop people in their tracks. Your first sentence must be gripping enough to pull them in, and your copy must continue to pull them in until they reach your call to action and resource box at the end.

Creating a Resource Box

When you create and distribute free articles online, consider your resource box your form of payment. Your resource box must work in tandem with your article to compel prospects to click to a page on your Website where they can either buy your products or learn more about your services.

Here are some tips:

> Create your resource box first. Decide what you want to promote (i.e., a product or a service) and create a page on your Website so you can link to it.

> Be certain the concept of your article ties in with what you are promoting in the resource box.

> Change your resource box and the page on your Website it links to in accordance with what your article promotes.

Submitting Your Articles

The Internet is filled with Websites that accept articles. Some Websites are "article banks" and others are owned by individuals or companies who like to offer their readers articles that relate to their mission. To find them, perform an Internet search for "article submission sites" and see the search results that suit your needs.

If you have a competitor who frequently writes online articles, you can perform a search of his name and words like "article" or "byline" and contact the Webmasters or owners of the sites he writes for.

You can also submit your article to the publishers of e-zines, but this is a time-consuming process. A smarter choice is to use a pay service such as *www.ezinetrendz.com* to distribute your articles to their proprietary list of e-zine publishers.

Syndicating Your Articles

You can also post articles on your own Website and syndicate them effortlessly by investing in a program called Master Syndicator (*www.mastersyndicator.com*). When people read your articles and want to post them on their site (with your resource information and a link to your site, of course), all they have to do is put two lines of JavaScript code on their page at the location where your content is to appear.

Creating a Compelling Signature File

Just as you spend serious time crafting and refining your elevator speech when you attend networking events, you will generate traffic to your Website and attract potential clients and customers when you create a mesmerizing signature file. A signature file is text (up to four to six lines) placed at the end of an e-mail message with the sender's contact information, Website address, or a tantalizing "call to action" hot-linked to a specific page on their Website.

Understanding the Power of a Signature File

In the real world, strangers, clients, and everyday folk we pass on the street size us up and make judgments based on our cars, clothes, and personal grooming. Potential clients judge us the same way, in addition to looking for external clues that would show our credibility. On the Internet, we are sized up by our helpfulness to others via e-mail or posting to an Internet discussion group. Posting solid information is essential.

Equally essential is topping that solid information off with the kind of signature file that motivates others to click on your hot-linked site and see what other goodies you have to offer.

Whether you are sending an e-mail to a prospect or posting an e-mail message to an entire mailing list, give thought to your signature file. No need to stick with a single file; you can change it at will. In Outlook 2000 and 2003, simply go to Tools (on the top navigation bar), scroll down to Options, and then select Mail Format to see the "Signatures" box at the bottom. (For other programs, use the "Help" option to find directions on creating a signature.)

Create a signature file(s) to suit what you want to promote. Some days, you may wish to promote a subscription to your e-zine, so in your e-mail you would create a "signature" with a link leading to a page on your Website where people can sign up for your e-zine, along with a compelling message of the benefits they would gain from subscription, especially if they act immediately.

For example, in one of my e-mail signatures I offer a free 36-page report on publicity when they sign up. In addition, the link in the signature leads to a page that offers them a sample of the e-zine and my privacy policy.

Feel free to promote anything in your signature, and change it at will to meet the objectives of whatever you are trying to accomplish by your e-mail or discussion group posting.

Discussion Forums Mark You as the Expert of Choice

One of the best ways to build your expertise on the Web is through discussion forums, also called newsgroups. Each discussion forum is made up of members who are interested in a specific niche topic. If a discussion forum is based on Yahoo or Topica, members have the option of receiving messages (called postings) by individual e-mail, or in a daily digest.

The objective here is to post helpful responses to people's questions, thus highlighting your expertise and including your signature line.

Begin finding appropriate discussion groups by visiting *groups.yahoo.com* or *www.topica.com* and plugging in words you would use to describe your niche, such as "publishing" or "sales and marketing." Then find the groups that have the largest members.

Monitor the discussions (called lurking) until you understand the group, and begin by politely answering a member's request for help. Be certain to include your signature line, but avoid any overt self-promotion. Members of the group are just getting to know you, and you want to give them the impression of being a polite, helpful expert.

E-zine as Sales Tool

To clients, customers, and prospects, your e-zine should be seen as a source of rich content and hard-to-find information they look forward to and voraciously tear into the moment it pops into their e-mail box. For them, it reinforces your value, underscores your expertise, and spreads positive word of mouth.

To you, your e-zine is a powerful promotional tool, allowing you to capture e-mail addresses of potential clients and customers so you can maintain top of the mind awareness and subtly soft sell them on a product or service in every issue.

Chances are you receive many e-zines, and barely have the time or inclination to open most of them. Yet perhaps there are a few that offer such excellent content you can't wait to rip them open.

To market yourself as a credible source of information, you must make an effort to produce the best e-zine you can and make sure you are providing value for your subscribers. Your e-zine does not have to be lengthy, but it should offer subscribers value, possibly in the form of:

> Easy-to-implement tips.

> Case studies or success stories.

> Examples of innovative techniques.

> A round up of articles or new books in your niche.

> Interviews with experts.

> Surveys (survey your niche market and report your findings to your subscribers).

> Guest articles (invite subscribers to share their experiences related to the theme of your e-zine).

Promoting Services and Products in Your E-zine

Many publishers of quality e-zines are also savvy promoters of their products and services. It's a good idea to develop a multitude of products so that you can offer a variety of fresh, exciting special offers with every issue. Furthermore, to maximize sales, tie the theme of your issue in with the product/ service you are trying to sell.

Note that the sales pitch should be subtle and low-key so it doesn't detract from the quality image you are trying to present. Your tone should be that of a person trying to solve a problem your subscriber wants to solve or information your subscriber needs via the product or service.

Keep a Personal Tone in Your E-zine

In addition to good, hard-to-find information, one of the most important elements of your e-zine is a warm, personal tone that reveals your personality. Even if a subscriber has never met you in person, they should find your "voice" and "presence" similar to the style of your writing.

People buy and use the services of people they like. Simply dispensing solid information fails to "brand" you so that you are seen in a different light than your competitors. The world is filled with people who perform similar services, and many of them have an e-zine.

As you prepare your draft issues, consider the ways you can show prospects how unique you truly are through a helpful, personal voice that makes people feel as though they are having a chat with a good friend.

E-zine Management

When you are growing your list, it is understandable you might not want to invest money in a professional e-zine distribution service until you have made money. As your list grows, so do your responsibilities, as you will have to personally handle unsubscribers and deal with other issues. Professional services can automate this process for you. Constant Contact (*www.constantcontact.com*) is free for less than 50 subscribers and may be a good place to start out, as it offers a variety of templates and you can see how many subscribers have actually opened your e-mail. I use a service called Sparklist (*www.Sparklist.com*) to manage an e-zine, which can be sent in plain text or HTML.

Autoresponder as Sales Tool

Autoresponders are automated e-mail messages. You have probably seen autoresponders in action when you have received an "out of the office" reply from someone to whom you had sent an e-mail.

When you use an autoresponder software program, you have the ability to send a series of messages to an individual, making it possible to send a free course by e-mail or keep top of the mind awareness of your services through a series of tips, prearranged to be sent out every few days or weeks as you prefer.

Let us assume you want to offer a free course to create top of the mind awareness among target customers. Your first choice would be to choose a free autoresponder, which means that an advertisement would be placed above the text of your autoresponder message. Your second choice is a fee-based autoresponder, which means you will have to pay a fee. (Note: You can find both by using "autoresponder" in an Internet search engine).

Next, you would load your course material into individual e-mail messages that would be delivered every day for five days, once a week for five weeks, or however you choose to arrange it.

In addition to educating your target audience about your products and services, autoresponders also give you the opportunity to "capture" the e-mail addresses of people who take the course, giving you the opportunity to market to them again.

Chapter Summary

1. Journalists find experts via a media or press room on your Website.

2. A running list of story ideas helps inspire journalists to write about you.

3. Choose domain names that are memorable, short, and easy to spell.

4. Your Web pages must load quickly, contain good navigation, and immediately inform visitors of benefits your site can offer them.

5. Consider selling your expertise from your Website in the form of downloadable or physical products.

6. Drive traffic to your site via keyword-rich Web pages.

7. Use online articles as a way of attracting visitors to your Website.

8. Posting helpful advice on discussion forums can help establish yourself as an expert and attract visitors.

9. Consider autoresponders as a way of staying in touch with prospects and offering automated information.

Chapter Assignments

☐ Build a media room on your site so that journalists can easily find information about you. To brainstorm ideas, visit the media rooms of experts in your field.

☐ Begin to create press releases and post them on your site.

☐ Brainstorm a domain name that may be shorter or more memorable than what you are using now. Brand yourself with it by switching from the e-mail address of your Internet provider (i.e., BillJones@msn.com) to your domain name (i.e., Bill@BillJones.com).

☐ If your business name is your domain name, get into the habit of using the ".com" extension as you speak of your business (i.e., MarketAbility.com instead of MarketAbility).

☐ Sell your intellectual property in physical and downloadable form from your Website. Look through your file cabinets for information you can repackage and sell on the Web.

☐ Ask friends and family to help you brainstorm keywords people would use to find the product or service you provide. Use these as keywords for specific pages on your site.

☐ Set up a schedule to go through your Website and make sure that each page has a specific purpose and unique keywords specific to that purpose.

☐ Write and syndicate articles to spread your name across the Net, as well as ones that will motivate people to click on the live link in your online resource box.

☐ Create a compelling signature line that will motivate people to click on your site for more information.

☐ Join discussion forums on the Internet to post helpful advice on the subject of your expertise, being sure to include your compelling signature line to motivate people to click on your site.

☐ Create an e-zine in order to compile a mailing list and keep in touch with clients and prospects.

☐ Use autoresponders as a way of giving automated information to prospects.

Resources and Recommended
_____Reading

Chapters 1 and 2: Basic Media Resources

Library Resources

Bacon's Media Directories.

Burrelle's Media Directory.

Gale Directory of Publications and Broadcast Media.

Chase's Calendar of Events.

Media Discs for Personal Use

Gebbie Press: The All-In-One Media Directory
   (_www.gebbieinc.com_).

Website

John Kremer's _Celebrate Today_ (_www.bookmarket.com_).

Chapters 3, 4, and 5: Publicity and Marketing Resources

Allen, Debbie. _Confessions of Shameless Self Promoters._

D'Vari, Marisa. "Media Magic: Grow Rich in Your Niche
   With Insider Media Secrets" (online course at
   www.BuildingBuzz.com).

Horowitz, Shel. *Grassroots Marketing: Getting Noticed in a Noisy World.*

Levinson, Jay Conrad, Rick Frishman, and Michael Larson. *Guerrilla Marketing for Writers.*

Levinson, Jay Conrad, Rick Frishman, and Jill Lublin. *Guerrilla Publicity.*

Michaels, Nancy, and Debbi Karpowicz. *Off-the-Wall Marketing Ideas.*

Michaels, Nancy. *Perfecting Your Pitch.*

Yudkin, Marcia. *6 Steps to Free Publicity.*

Radio and TV Resources

Radio-TV Interview Report (Website· *www.rtir.com*; Telephone: 1-800-989-1400, ext. 713).

"Gordon's Radio List" (*www.nrbooks.com/ radiopublicity.html*).

Bradley's Guide to the Top National TV Talk & Interview Shows (*www.freepublicity.com/getontoptv/ orderchoice.html*).

Alliance for Community Media (*www.alliancecm.org*).

Chapter 6: Networking Resources

Andre, Mary Lou. *Ready to Wear: An Expert's Guide to Choosing and Using Your Wardrobe.*

Boothman, Nicholas. *How to Connect in Business in 90 Seconds or Less.*

Danielson, Diane. *Table Talk.*

Darling, Diane. *The Networking Survival Guide.*

Horn, Sam. *Tongue Fu!: How to Deflect, Disarm, and Defuse Any Verbal Conflict.*

RoAne, Susan. *How to Work a Room*.

Rosen, Emanuel. *The Anatomy of Buzz*.

Chapter 7: Writing and Publishing Resources

Appelbaum, Judith. *How to Get Happily Published*.

Atchity, Kenneth. *A Writer's Time*.

Bowerman, Peter. *The Well-Fed Writer*.

Burgett, Gordon. *Publishing to Niche Markets*.

D'Vari, Marisa. *Creating Characters: Let Them Whisper Their Secrets*.

D'Vari, Marisa. *Script Magic: Subconscious Techniques to Conquer Writer's Block*.

Kremer, John. *1001 Ways to Market Your Books*.

Larsen, Michael. *How to Write a Book Proposal*.

Lyon, Elizabeth. *Nonfiction Book Proposals Anybody Can Write*.

Poynter, Dan. *The Self-Publishing Manual: How to Write, Print, and Sell Your Own Book, 14th Edition*.

Reiss, Fern. *The Publishing Game series*.

Ross, Marilyn. *Shameless Marketing for Brazen Hussies: 307 Awesome Money-Making Strategies for Savvy Entrepreneurs*.

Ross, Tom and Marilyn. *Jump Start Your Book Sales*.

Ross, Tom and Marilyn. *The Complete Guide to Self-Publishing*.

Sansevieri, Penny. *Get Published Today!*

Additional Publishing Resources

Publishers Weekly (trade magazine).

Publishers Marketing Association (*www.pma-online.org*).

Literary Marketplace (a library reference).

www.TipsBooklets.com (booklet information).

Chapter 8: Public Speaking Resources

D'Vari, Marisa. *Presentation Magic: Dazzle & Deliver Talks With Confidence.*

Dieken, Connie. Audiotapes at *www.CommunicateLikeAPro.com.*

www.ipl.org/div/subject/browse/ref09.00.00 (to find associations).

Chapter 9: Writing Resources

Kawa-Jump, Shirley. *How to Publish Your Articles.*

McCabe-Cardoza, Monica. *You Can Write a Column.*

Sedge, Michael. *Successful Syndication.*

Chapter 10: Online Promotion Resources

Cohen, June. *The Unusually Useful Web Book.*

Krug, Steve. *Don't Make Me Think.*

Nielsen, Jakob. *Designing Web Usability.*

O'Keefe, Steve. *Complete Guide to Internet Publicity.*

Rose, M.J. and Angela Adair-Hoy. *How to Publish and Promote Online.*

Yudkin, Marcia. *Internet Marketing for Less Than $500/Year.*

A

"about the author," 145-146
acronyms, 92, 112
action plan, developing, 82-83
agents, 147-148, 151-152
Allen, Debbie, 68, 109, 117, 122, 138, 160
Andre, Mary Lou, 22, 76, 78, 115-116, 118-119, 124, 135
Annie Jennings PR, 94-95
anxiety, calming, 179
appearances, 76-79, 120
Appelbaum, Judith, 142, 149
articles, 168, 195-211, 216-218, 230-233
associations, contacting, 167
attachments, 42, 203
audiences, 53-54, 61-74, 129, 180, 190-191
autoresponders, 238-239

B

back cover copy, 143-144
Bacon's, 47, 87

beat reporters, 54-55
behavior, on-air, 111-112
body language, 103-104, 137
book proposals, 146-148
book, writing a, 133-163
booklets, 161
books, to establish niche and brand, 135-137, 209
books, alternatives to, 161
Bowerman, Peter, 138, 185
brainstorming, 27-28, 80, 92, 100, 121
brand, establishing, 135-137
budgets, 109
building buzz, definition, 21
business cards, 126-127

C

cable access interview tips, 90
Caine, Ken Winston, 144, 152, 154-156
calendar, editorial, 201
call-in shows, 63

Canfield, Jack, 136, 185
CDs, audio, 186
Celebrate Today, 36
Chase's Calendar of Events,
    36, 69, 81
Chicken Soup for the Soul,
    136, 185
clothing, 110, 124-125, 130
CNN, 76, 78, 142
Communicate Like a Pro, 108
competition, analyzing, 147
*Complete Guide to Self-
    Publishing, The,* 157
*Confessions of Shameless Self
    Promoters,* 68, 109, 117,
    122, 138, 160
confidence, enhancing, 179
cover copy, back, 143-144
Covey, Stephen R., 44
creative license, 140
credibility, 98, 133, 220-223
Cunningham, Bill, 82-83

D

Darling, Diane, 51, 166
demo video, 88-89
DePalma, Tami, 86, 220
Dieken, Connie, 102, 108
directories, media, 47-48
discussion forums, 235
domain extensions, using, 220
Donlan, Vicki, 116, 122-123

downloads, immediate, 226
Driscoll, Marilee, 75, 76,
    185, 224
Dushinski, Kim, 220

E

e-books, 187
editing, the value of, 140, 147
editor, letters to the, 205-206
editorial calendar, 201
e-mail pitch, 40, 42, 65
e-mail query letter, 151
e-mail release headlines, 45
Emerson Consulting Group,
    Inc., 152, 167, 196
emotion, creating, 108, 180
Encyclopedia of Associations,
    167, 191
etiquette, business card,
    126-127
excitement, generating, 71
e-zines, 235-238

F

filler material, 30-31
financial indices, 32-33
follow-up calls, 46-47, 93
forums, discussion, 235
freebies, 67, 71
Fuhrman, John, 133, 184

G

Get Published Today!,
140, 166
ghostwriters, 158-160
Godek, Greg, 22, 88
Gordon, William A., 65-67, 74
Greengard, Sam, 56-57
Grundfest, Joseph, 32

H

Hansen, Mark, 136, 185
headlines, 43-45, 202
Hersey, William D., 128
holidays, creating, 36-38
hook, developing a, 25-50,
80-82
How to Work a Room, 19, 116
Hug Your Cat Day, 36

I

image, creating a, 124-125
indices, financial, 32-33
Internet, 39
interviewing, 57-59, 99-102,
105-106, 109-110
interview, radio, 61-74
interview, television, 75-95
introduction, attention-
getting, 177-178
inverted pyramid style, 46

J

jargon, 112
Jennings, Annie, 94-95
journalists, 59
Jud, Brian, 89

K

Karpowicz, Debbi, 134-135
keywords, 227, 228-230
Klensch, Elsa, 78
Kremer, John, 36

L

LaCroix, Darren, 184, 187,
188, 224
Larsen, Michael, 148
Laskowski, Lenny, 138
late-night talk shows, 35
Lesonsky, Rieva, 119
letters to the editor, 205-206
letters, query, 148-151
Lindauer, Lois, 118
listening skills, 126, 130
Lit From Within, 109
Literary Marketplace, 152
Lizotte, Ken, 167, 196-197

M

magnet events, 134-135
Mailer, Norman, 89

makeup, 110
market, target, 52-53
MarketAbility.com, 86, 220
marketing, 115-131, 191
Martinson, Connie, 89
Mayer, Margery, 136
McCall, Kimberly, 62
McGarvey, Robert, 56-57
media attention, luring, 134
media contacts, 47-49, 51-60
media directories, 47-48
media kits, 85, 86-89
media parties, 134-135
media room, 214-218
media training, 97-113
message, packaging and
    selling your, 101-102
Michaels, Nancy, 119- 120,
    129, 135, 173
Michaud, Julie, 51
Mitchell, Nancy, 51
Mohyde, Colleen, 147-148
momentum, building, 71,
    153-154
Montelongo, Paul, 199
Moran, Victoria, 109
Morgan, Rebecca, 61-62,
    76-77
Munier, Paula, 147

Nelson, Bruce, 119
Nelson, Rick, 203-205
Network World, 203
networking resistance,
    confronting, 117-118
*Networking Survival Guide,
    The,* 51, 166
networking techniques,
    creative, 115-131
New York Times, 52, 171,
    199, 205, 206
news hook, 80-82
news release, 38-46
newspapers, 27-28, 52
niche market, finding your,
    119, 135-137
Norton, Bob, 171

O

O'Berry, Denise, 123, 125
Ogilvy, David, 43, 170
on-air behavior, 111-112
online articles, 230-233
online media kit, 85
online promotion, 213-241
opinion pieces, writing, 205
Oprah Winfrey Show, The,
    26, 76, 79, 81

N

names, remembering, 128
Nathan, Jan, 139

P

partnerships, 124
pause, power of the, 104, 183

pay for placement, 79, 94-95
Perfecting Your Pitch, 22,
    119, 129, 135, 174
phone scripts, 46-47, 93
physical gestures, 182
pitch, creating a, 42, 53-54,
    63, 65, 84-85, 87-88, 90-93
Plante, Thomas, Ph.D., 141
platform, building your, 22-23
posture, 111, 128
Poynter, Dan, 143-144,
    152-154, 226
presentations, developing
    and delivering, 175
press releases, 94, 215
print media, how to get
    interviewed by, 51-60
Print-On-Demand, 139-143
producers, pitching to, 64-67
promotions, online, 213-241
proposal, book, 146-148
public speaking, 165-193
publishers, 151-152
Publishing Game, The, 136
publishing, traditional vs.
    self, 138

Q

Qubein, Nido, 180
query letters, 148-151, 201-202
questions, handling interview,
    106-107
Quinn, Robin, 158

R

radio interviews, 61-74
radio pitchs, customizing, 63
radio producers, pitching,
    64-67
radio shows, call-in, 63
radio, media training for, 109
Radio-TV Interview Report,
    67-68, 69, 73
Reiss, Fern, 136, 138, 171
reporters, contacting, 54-55,
resistance, confronting
    networking, 117-118
resource box, creating, 232
retailers, secure online, 227
retention, 181, 182
RoAne, Susan, 17-19, 116-117
Rodale, 144, 154
role-playing, 107
Rosen, Emanuel, 124
Ross, Marilyn, 157
Ross, Tom, 157
Roth, Eileen, 26, 79-80

S

sales letters, 144-145
Sansevieri, Penny C., 140-141,
Schurr, Amy, 203
Schwalbe, Will, 151
Scott, Gini Graham, 151
scripts, phone, 46-47, 93

Secrets of Savvy Networking, The, 18
self-promotion, 21
self-publishing, 138-141, 152
selling, 101-102, 188
seminars, 171-173
Sena, Kathy, 56-57
Sheldon, Sidney, 89
Shields, Dave, 73
signature file, 233-234
Singer, Jen, 198-199
6 Steps to Free Publicity, 117
smiling, 111, 128, 130
Soul Proprietor, 224
sound bites, 99, 107, 108
speaking events, 167, 168, 171-172, 183-184
speaking, public, 165-193
speech writing, 169, 175-176
story ideas, creating, 26-36
sub-headlines, 45
subject lines, 41
surveys, 33-34, 175
syndication, 206-208, 233

T

target audience, 52-54, 61-74,
telephone script, 46-47
television interviews, 75-95
television pitches, 84, 87-88, 90-93
Tessina, Tina, 55
tip sheet, 30-31

Toastmasters, 81, 165, 184, 187, 224
Today, 26, 79, 81
touch marketing, 129
trade publications, 34
training, media, 97-113
transformation, books as tools of, 135
transition points, 181

V

Vasiliadis, Chris, 125, 209
Ventrice, Cindy, 135-136, 138, 157
videos, demo, 88-89, 187
visualization, 24, 120-121
vocal variation, 64, 181-182

W

Wall Street Journal, 51, 52, 151, 171, 206, 213
Websites, 219-225, 227-228
Well-Fed Writer, The, 138, 185
Wilson, Jane, 126-127
Writer's Market, 152, 200
writing, 133-163, 168, 199-205

Y

Yudkin, Marcia, 117, 224

About the Author

Founder of Deg.Com Communications, **Marisa D'Vari** empowers entrepreneurs, executives, and corporations through media positioning and presentation skills. She has worked as an executive in the entertainment and media industries for more than a decade.

A national speaker and author of five books to date, D'Vari conducts keynote speeches and workshops for a wide variety of corporations and associations, including the Institute of Management Consultants, the American Society of Association Executives, the National Speakers Association, Boston Security Analysts Society, and Harvard University.

To contact D'Vari with regard to consulting, training, or speaking, e-mail her at mdvari@BuildingBuzz.com. She is based in both Manhattan and Los Angeles.

D'Vari offers complimentary articles, reports, and a biweekly e-zine on her Website, *www.BuildingBuzz.com*, and encourages you to contact her via e-mail with personal stories of your success for future books and articles.